Through stories of a 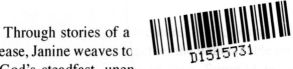 disease, Janine weaves to of God's steadfast, unen paralyzed by our fears, but Janine learned from the incredible women, children, and men of Zimbabwe to face fears with the strength and faith that come only from the one who promises to never leave us alone. By reading this book, you are honoring the beautiful lives of God's people.

— Rev. Melissa Maher
Pastor of Serving Ministry
Chapelwood United Methodist Church

Janine Roberts dared to love the people of Zimbabwe completely through her ministry, her witness, and her person. Now she dares to love the readers of this book completely by sharing her story in such a personal and vivid way that we too can be amazed and appalled, joyous and brokenhearted, here and yet there. She is the voice of the voiceless to those who have ears willing to hear. Thank You, Lord, for calling her; thank you, Janine, for saying yes.

— Rev. Rob Mehner
Spiritual Formation Pastor
La Croix Church

Over the years, Janine's newsletters have captured the missionary moment so well that I have cried over them, used them in sermons, and used them in class. Now she has written a book showing us the face of God's mission in the HIV/AIDS epidemic that affects more than one-fourth of the population of Zimbabwe. It is a crisis for children, for caregivers, for families, and for the church; that is, the whole church worldwide. Why should we care? Because God cares—and because God cares, Janine serves as the face of Jesus for many who are suffering and dying (2 Corinthians 4:6–7).

—Dr. Michael Rynkiewich
Professor of Anthropology
Asbury Seminary

Janine has provided a unique treatment of a subject very close to my heart. Her writing is reflective, touching, and challenging in many different ways. I cannot overstate my admiration for her prayerful and practical approach to the real-life experiences of those infected and affected by HIV/AIDS in Zimbabwe, my home country. This emphasis gives the book an exceptional ability to capture the reader's mind in an amazing way. *Dare to Love Completely* is a must-read for any person who wants to make a difference in the lives of people anywhere in the world. The content of this book is best summarized by the words from Isaiah 40:31: "Those who hope in the LORD will renew their strength. They will soar on wings like eagles; they will run and not grow weary, they will walk and not be faint."

—Monicah Muhomba, PhD
Vanderbilt University

Dare to Love Completely

A Memoir from Zimbabwe

Janine Roberts

Dare to Love Completely
A Memoir from Zimbabwe
by Janine Roberts

Printed in the United States of America

ISBN 978-1-61579-018-0

www.xulonpress.com

Seek His right future
possibilities! "Thy
Kingdom come." Peace
be with you and yours!
　　　　Wenyu Munashe!

　　　　Janine
　　　　Roberts

*G*o to the end of the path until you get to the gate. Go through the gate and head straight out towards the horizon. Keep going towards the horizon. Sit down and have a rest every now and again, but keep on going. Just keep on with it. Keep on going as far as you can. That's how you get there.

—Anonymous

For Shingi

Contents

Preface

"They say there is light at the end of every tunnel. Unfortunately, for Zimbabwe, it is behind us." This is a statement I once heard a man say as we stood looking out among a seemingly endless line of cars waiting to collect our precious few liters of fuel during yet another shortage.

I have been walking down one of these tunnels for the past few years alongside the men, women, and children of beautiful Zimbabwe, Africa. As we walked farther in, our eyes began to adjust to the darkness, and we were able to keep going. After a while, we each came to a place of almost total darkness. It was at this point I began to notice a small glow coming from a few of the people until we could see enough to begin walking again.

This glow is the tiny spark of hope God has placed inside each one of us. Seeing it in others causes our own spark to flame, and we are able to keep going. There have been times while living in Zimbabwe I could feel my own flame begin to dim. Sometimes it felt like it had gone out completely, but there was always a hand to take hold of mine to lead the way until my flame ignited again.

That flame of hope is what I pray you will see in each of the people in this book. A lot of suffering, struggle, and darkness have occurred in this culture that may be very different from anything you have ever known, but you might also begin to recognize the similarities that hold true throughout humanity. We are all faced with times of suffering, struggle, and darkness in our lives. I hope that something in this book resonates so that you remember during those times to grab hold of someone's hand and just wait for your eyes to adjust.

Jesus is familiar with all our sufferings. He is the calm in each of our struggles and the light leading us in our darkness. I don't know what is at the end of this tunnel, but we all must keep walking forward with certainty because God does know, and He is good.

I have heard it said that our lives should be a book about Jesus. This is a book about Jesus, written to show how He worked in just a few people's lives within only a few years. "Jesus did many other things as well. If every one of them were written down, I suppose that even the whole world would not have room for the books that would be written" (John 21:25).

Let this small testimony act as a reminder to never give up. Each of the stories in this book is written as true as my memory can record them. Some names have been changed in order to respect privacy.

Wenyu Munashe (Yours in Christ),
Janine Roberts

Acknowledgments

The title for this book came many years ago in Zimbabwe while I was eating a Dove dark chocolate candy with a little saying on the wrapper (since that very first trip with Tiffany, there has always been a little chocolate stashed in my suitcase). Thank you, Tiffany, for taking the first step with me, and thank you to St. Paul's for sending us.

To Christie, Anna, Nicole, Emily, Lynn, Melissa, Julia, Liz and any other woman brave enough to live among the spiders with me, I admire each one of you.

I would like to thank Reverend Royals who pointed me in the direction of Asbury, where I met lifelong friends and where the professors helped shape and grow my faith through their example. To all my Asbury girls, well, there just aren't words, but you know what I mean.

Thank you to my editor, Brenda Pitts, whose kind words gave me the courage to actually send this book to the publisher.

Thanks to CornerStone, who was willing to take a chance on a single girl. You built me up, sent me out, and when I came home a crying mess, you built me back up and sent me out again. That sounds like genuine love. You are a true blessing to me.

Thank you to each person who has supported the Project HOPE children and families through your prayers, gifts, and service, and thank you to FOSA, who gave the Fairfield children a real family. May you all receive blessing upon blessing from your Father in heaven.

Of course, I would never be complete without my entire family's solid love and support. Thank you, Josh, for being the best little "brudder" ever and coming to visit me. Thank you, Dad and Mom, for loving me so much you were willing to let me go. I do realize the sacrifices you have made for me. I love you.

Lastly, I acknowledge each of my children, some of whom have already danced into the arms of their Savior. This book is an outpouring of my love for you, but greater still is the love of your Father. Not for one moment have you ever truly been orphans. You are the sons and daughters of the King.

Chapter 1

Dream Fulfilled

*I've dreamt in my life dreams that have
stayed with me ever after.*
—Emily Bronte
Wuthering Heights

I'm not sure when the idea first came to me, but I do remember the day it became a possibility. My cousin Tiffany and I were playing with Barbies in the basement of her house. I realize looking back that we were both far too old to still be playing with Barbies. My cousin was already in the sixth grade, and I was born two years before her, so I'll let you do the math. The exact order of the conversation has become unclear, but one of us asked the question "If you could travel anywhere, where would you want to go?" My answer was immediate: Africa. My cousin's wishes echoed my own, and we decided at that moment that one day we would go. It started as simply as that.

We didn't really care where in Africa we went or what we would do when we got there. There seemed to be something mysterious and intriguing about the continent that drew our interest. A few years later, a woman from our church gave a talk about her mission trip to Russia. We were immediately captivated by her experiences. She gave us a brochure that I still have in my mounds of "important and highly necessary keepsakes" that told of groups going all over the world to do mission work. There was one section with a highlighted map of Africa that caught our attention right away. A team went on a three-week trip once a year to assist people in a country called Zimbabwe.

Neither of us had ever heard of Zimbabwe, but soon Tiffany and I became fixated on the place described in the pages of that document: desperate-looking orphans; little clay and straw huts; safaris in the bush to spot giraffes, zebras, and lions; and a great stretch of waterfalls known as Victoria Falls, creating one of the seven natural wonders of the world. At seventeen and fifteen years of age, we became determined to go to a country that had previously been unknown to us, located at the bottom of a continent that was planted firmly in our hearts for reasons we could not explain.

For the next few years, our parents rarely heard a pause in our constant pleas and petitions. We now had a valid argument and did everything in our power to convince them to agree with us. Surely they would want us to go to Africa if it meant helping orphans. What would they do without our help? We, of course, downplayed the two safaris and the trip to Victoria Falls, which were also featured as a perk at the end of the expedition. In a final moment of weakness, our parents relented. None of them thought we would actually follow through.

By January of the following year, however, we were still fiercely determined. Momentum increased as church members began potlucks, garage sales, and various other functions to raise the money we would need. I was a junior in college at the time. Tiffany was finishing her senior year of high school in our hometown. We were caught up in a whirlwind of excitement, not really knowing anymore what was happening. Each time a payment was due, there would be just enough money to cover the expense. When the final statement came, we had to put in only seventy-five dollars of our own money. The next day, a woman from our church invited us for a visit, and when we got up to leave, she handed each of us a hundred-dollar bill. After that the money stopped flowing just as quickly as it had begun. It was my first lesson in trusting God to provide for me. He had given us just enough—no more, no less. Tiffany and I were going to Africa, and I will remain forever grateful that I had someone who shared my dream.

Before I knew it, there were only three days before our plane left for Zimbabwe, and Tiffany and I were ready. Our suitcases were filled to overflowing with only the "bare necessities" for traveling to a foreign country. We had plenty of candy and chocolate, dried fruits in case we were lost somewhere in the wilderness, and lots of cute sleeveless shirts and shorts to help us tan in the African sun. We did not realize we would be stepping off the plane into an African winter. July is the coldest month of the year in Zimbabwe, and although it was nothing compared to the snowy days in the West Virginia mountains where we grew up, the drop to fifty degrees at night during our trip would still shock our systems. There was no central heating in Zimbabwe.

We had a long flight before we would arrive at that point, however. First we boarded a chartered bus, meeting the others on our team and receiving an assigned number. Throughout the rest of the journey, each time we gathered, the numbers were sounded aloud one through twenty-five to make sure all were present. Fortunately, none of us were ever lost. This was helped by the fact that we were all forced into wearing bright purple T-shirts with oversized collars.

After the initial pleasantries, we settled in for the nine-hour drive to Detroit, only to find our flight delayed once we arrived. Finally making it to London on only a few hours of sleep, we toured the city by double-decker bus, watching the cars speed past on the left side of the road.

Back on board for the final flight to Zimbabwe, we were now exhausted. My energy returned quickly the moment we landed a mere ten hours later. With the sun rising just as we stepped off the plane, I felt all my childhood dreams being realized as my foot touched African ground for the first time. We exchanged our money at the airport bank: twenty-eight Zim dollars for every one U.S. dollar. It was time to start the journey to our final destination.

For the next few hours, I fought sleep, trying with everything in me to keep my eyes opened and focused on my first sights of Africa. This was helped by the fact that we were all lumped together on a very small bus, bumping over large potholes every few minutes. There were huge stones sitting in the middle of open fields, stacked oddly on top of one another, looking as if they were about to topple over. *Zimbabwe* means "big house of stones," and I could now see why it was given the name.

The most beautiful thing about the country, however, was not the landscape, but the people. Small children raced down dirt paths on the side of the road. The colors of their uniforms were diverse, each signifying a different school. Mothers carried babies on their backs, held by a piece of cloth that wrapped firmly around the mothers' waists. Out of small thatched-roof huts, women and men went to and fro, wearing brightly colored clothing.

We arrived three hours later at Africa University, where we would be staying for the following weeks. The college students were on break for the semester, and Tiffany and I found ourselves in a dorm room only slightly bigger than the shoebox I had to endure in my freshman year of college. After a very good night's sleep, we awoke the next morning to prepare for a tour of the campus. As we walked, I saw two Zimbabwean women bent over in the fields working. Behind them rose large mountains framed by the bright green of the field below. It was perfect. It was what I had always imagined Africa would be.

That same day, Tiffany and I learned our first words of Shona from a friend who joined us at the cafeteria dinner table, where we sat eating chicken and rice. (Shona is the main tribal language spoken in Zimbabwe.) Over 75 percent of the population speaks Shona, although the official language taught in schools is English. We were eager to learn as much of this second language as we could. Although I didn't understand the importance at the time, I would later find out that speaking to others in their own language, or even attempting to learn a few words, speaks so strongly of love to them. It shows a desire to know their culture, which makes up a large part of who they are.

As the very first fumbled syllables rolled off my tongue, I began to fall in love with the Shona culture. This was one of the first ways God started planting within me a strong desire to truly know Zimbabwe and its people. My first words that day would be written down in my journal, practiced, and throughout the years bring smiles to the faces of hundreds of Zimbabweans as they heard my funny accent. *Mangwanani* meant "good morning," *masikati* meant "good afternoon," and *manheru* meant "good evening." The final word we learned for the day was *mazviita,* the ever-important "thank you." There was now a small piece of Shona culture that belonged to me.

That night Tiffany and I managed to get through to our parents on a giant telephone box located outside one of the buildings on campus. (I am sure my dad had to take out a small loan to pay off the phone bills from the calls we placed during our trip.) Just before bedtime, we held our first nightly devotions as a team. The woman leading the devotional time asked us to write on a piece of paper what we wanted to accomplish during the trip. We then placed these requests into a basket one by one, giving our talents to God. As I released my hope for this trip, I had to wonder what exactly might be in store.

Another woman from our team stood up at the end and sang in the most enchanting voice. The words would forever remain engraved in my memory, and I would repeat them through tear-filled eyes each time I returned to Zimbabwe in the years to come. The struggle would always ensue, as the comfortable and familiar of home battled with the challenge and anticipation of leaving. But these words would put my feet into motion, as with a deep breath I left my family behind and passed through the ever-increasing security at the airport checkpoint. Looking back every few moments until my mom, dad, and brother became tiny specks waving good-bye, I would sing to myself:

> I'll go, Lord, I'll go. I'll go, Lord, I'll go.
> If the Lord needs somebody, here am I, Lord, send me.
> Though I be motherless, I'll go.
> Though I be fatherless, Lord, I'll go.
> If the Lord needs somebody, here am I, Lord, send me.

Though I be friendless, I'll go.
Though I be friendless, Lord, I'll go.
If the Lord needs somebody, here am I, Lord,
    send me.

*   *   *   *   *

The next day was Sunday, and after a short bus ride, we were herded like cattle into a church that had a dirt floor, only three walls, and no ceiling. There were rough wooden benches with no backs standing in rows inside the small enclosure. Tiffany and I were quickly shoved into an already tightly packed row. People continued to stream in until the church was overflowing and people were standing outside.

Before I knew what was happening, the room began to fill with heavenly voices. Something went straight to my soul and settled there. The rhythm and sounds echoed inside me like a steady drumbeat, as the singing grew louder and louder. The woman beside me handed Tiffany and me a well-used hymnbook, and we desperately tried to follow the jumble of Shona words on the page, but in the end I gave up and just stood there, letting the sounds envelop me. As they sang, the energy rose in the room until everyone was shouting and dancing. I had never seen God fill people with so much energy and joy. They had a spirit inside of them that surrounded everything until it became almost tangible. In the middle of this dilapidated building with no roof, as a light rain began to fall, all they were focused on was praising their Father.

A man rose, went to the front, and began preaching in a loud voice. As everyone else listened intently to the Shona words, I took the opportunity to steal a few glances at the people around me. A woman with a brightly colored cloth tied around her waist as a skirt and another wrapped tightly around her head swayed back and forth slightly in her seat as she agreed with each word the pastor spoke. A frail old man in a tattered suit leaned heavily on his walking stick planted firmly in front of him, both hands resting gently on top. He had a quiet dignity about him, earned by age and perhaps unspoken hardships. There was a small baby, clothed in a green crocheted outfit complete with a matching hat, seated on his mother's lap. With a grin on his face, he gazed at this strange new face beside him, lips slightly quivering only when I tried to reach out to hold him.

Next in the service, a table was moved to the front where the preacher had been standing. It was time to give an offering, and I wondered for a moment if anyone here would have anything to give. But the whole room rose in what seemed to be a single motion, as every person joined the line that was now forming and danced to the front to lay down their gifts. This was an opportunity to give back to the one who had provided for them.

The pastor then sent us off with a benediction, and instantly people swarmed around us, wanting to know our names, where we had come from, why we were there. I was humbled and overwhelmed by their automatic and sincere welcome.

Later that afternoon, we traveled around the nearby town of Mutare, stopping at an overlook that divided Mozambique from Zimbabwe. Even from atop the mountain, we could tell the two countries had entirely different landscapes. The ground dropped steeply into a valley on the Zimbabwean side, where small buildings and houses dotted the land. As we drove back down into this valley, we entered a high-density area, packed with people streaming through the streets. Vendors were selling fruit, and laundry hung from the back of small, crowded shacks.

This was Sakubva, one of the most impoverished and densely occupied areas around Mutare. As any good American tourist, I took out my camera, snapped one picture, but instantly felt ashamed. This was real life. It wasn't meant to be a main attraction. I silently pushed my camera back inside my bag and wondered how I would feel if my life were on display from someone's tour bus.

As we awoke that third morning, ready to start our week of work at Old Mutare Mission, I had no idea that my life was about to be forever changed. We waited for our driver, who finally arrived and took us the few miles from Africa University to the orphanage at Old Mutare, an area of land where a church, school, and hospital had been built over a hundred years earlier. As we passed the large church near the front of the mission, I began to feel anxious. Winding on until we reached the end of the dirt road, far back from the main entrance, we left the safety of the car and headed toward our destination: Fairfield Orphanage. This was it. All those desperate orphans would be waiting inside for us to just swoop in and save the day.

As we opened the front door, however, our determination wavered. The smell of urine overwhelmed us as we took in the sight of dozens of old rusted cribs lined side by side against the walls. The children ran toward us instantly, clinging, grabbing, and climbing. A wave of nausea took away any grandiose ideas I had of saving the world. I was doing good just to stay upright. We managed to make it to the outside courtyard, children still holding fast to every arm and leg we had to offer.

As the fresh air of the courtyard swept over us, the smells neutralized and we managed to breathe a little easier. I quickly found my first baby to love. Mildred, a one-year-old girl, wore a pink sweater and skirt and held tightly to me, as if she never wanted to let go. She clung to me with a trust that a child gives only to its mother, fully surrendering herself as her head came to rest against me. Surrounding us were children running and screaming in every direction, their laughter overshadowing their dirty faces and threadbare clothes. Others were sitting on the ground, sullen and quiet.

As I looked around at the chaos unfolding before me, I realized why Mildred had so quickly accepted me and why she was so apprehensive for me to let her go. This was her one short-lived chance at having someone to specifically pay attention to her. Once I put her down, she would again be swept away in the mayhem all around her.

After a while, one of the workers handed me a small bowl, making gestures for me to feed one of the babies. We found out that the children ate the same meal every day: ground corn and water boiled together into a mixture called *sadza*. Resembling grits, it is the staple food for every meal in Zimbabwe. I sat cross-legged in front of another one-year-old, who hungrily ate every bite until his little belly puffed out.

A few minutes later, two girls walked out into the courtyard and introduced themselves as being volunteers from America. Anna and Christie were from Nebraska and were now spending the year in Zimbabwe, working with the children at Fairfield Orphanage. They were having tiny toilets installed for the children, which we could tell were much needed after seeing the hole in the ground at the side of the courtyard that the children were currently using.

Tiffany and I left the children a while later and followed Christie and Anna to see the babies. Children under one year of age were kept in cribs placed side by side in one of the hospital rooms next door to the orphanage. The babies would lie in their cribs all day long, rarely being held or touched. A nurse would come in once every three hours to feed and change them. Then they would be left alone once again. Tiffany and I picked up each of the babies in turn and played with them.

When Tiffany went toward a baby lying on the corner cot, Anna stopped her, warning that she would need to wear gloves when holding the child. Grace was smaller than all the other babies, although she was one of the oldest. She was HIV positive, and we could now see sores all over her body. Tiffany did not pick her up. I did not pick her up. It was Amanda, a sixteen-year-old and the youngest of our team members, who placed a plastic glove on each hand, wrapped the baby in a blanket, and gently held her, rocking her back and forth. When Amanda turned to me and asked if I wanted to hold Grace, I didn't answer her. Instead, I turned and walked away in shameful silence.

Knowing all the facts about how AIDS was transmitted, I logically understood that I could not catch the disease, but coming face-to-face with it for the first time, I was suddenly struck with a terrible sense of fear I couldn't explain. I could no longer see the small baby before me, but only the death and disease that seemed to surround her. I was not ready to face the reality of what it would mean to hold Grace, to perhaps chance falling in love with this child who had already begun the process of dying. God was beside me in that moment, willing me to see this child through His eyes. He loved her so much. I vowed silently as we left the building that day that I would hold Grace before I left Zimbabwe.

Chapter 2

Gifts of Grace

I am no longer my own, but thine.
—John Wesley
Book of Offices of the
British Methodist Church

It was now lunchtime, and I suddenly began to feel sick and sullen. I could hardly manage to lift the food to my mouth. Everything I had seen that morning began to hit me, and I did not want to enter the orphanage again. I was in my first throes of culture shock. What I was experiencing in this new culture was so different from anything I had known in the comfortable familiarity of home that I physically could not handle it. Tiffany was good at sensing that something was wrong, so after lunch we opted to take a walk to the church we had passed on our way in earlier. It loomed large against the backdrop of the mountains surrounding the mission. As we approached, a groundskeeper came and kindly offered to show us the inside. We walked through the large hall, amazed at the towering ceiling of this simple concrete building, colorful banners hanging from its walls.

When we reached the front of the sanctuary, I handed the man a tiny pocket Bible to thank him for showing us around. As he took it, his other hand reached up and pushed the hat back from his forehead. His eyes glistened over and he sat down, throwing his head back and his broom to the ground as he mumbled something in Shona. He opened the book slowly and ran his fingers across the words. His eyes closed, and he kept saying, *"Mazviita, mazviita, Mwari"* (Thank You, thank You, God), one of the only phrases I had learned.

The Gideons passed those small Bibles out every year at my college. Half the students wouldn't even take them, and I had seen many throwing them away. I could not convey how spoiled and materialistic I felt at that moment. This man had received a precious gift, and I cried with him as I began to realize how distorted my view of the world had been up to this point.

Gaining courage from this man, I took a deep breath and returned to the orphanage. My new friend Nyarai, a five-year-old I had met earlier, wanted to be held. Throughout the afternoon, we laughed and danced our way to music coming from a small radio. Her smile lit me up inside each time she pointed to her stomach and said yes, waiting to be tickled.

I brought her into the small kitchen attached to the courtyard and searched through my bag for my one remaining mint. When we went back outside, a boy named Moses began crying hysterically over his lack of mints. Seeing his large round eyes fill with tears, I instantly felt guilty for not having more to offer. I watched as Nyarai immediately split the mint with her teeth and placed half in the open mouth of the sobbing boy. Nyarai had no material possessions of her own but was willing to share half of what she had been given to stop Moses from being sad. God spoke to me in that moment, and I realized I would someday return to Fairfield Orphanage to stay and learn from His children.

For now, however, my system was still in shock from all the new experiences. I avoided the orphanage the next few days, choosing instead to work with the men on our team as they helped to build one of the staff houses at the university. Tiffany and I spent all morning swinging bricks, a technique in which we all stood in a line and swung one brick after another to the next person in the row. The bricks moved down the line in this way until they reached their destination. We had just made a nice-sized pile when the foreman came and told us we had moved the bricks to the wrong spot. We would have to put them back.

Each night I fell into bed exhausted, wondering why I could not make myself go back to the orphanage. There were only a few days left with the children, but something inside me now knew I would be coming back, and it was too much to process. If I thought about what that really meant, I knew I would shut down. This place was too different; it would be too hard.

After three days of avoiding the place, Tiffany and I headed back to Old Mutare Mission. For the last few days, we would help at the crèche (preschool) on the opposite side of the property from the orphanage. At the far left of the mission stood the hospital and the orphanage, while the primary school, church, and secondary school stood in the middle. Passing all that, we finally came to the crèche. There was a surprise waiting for me as we went through the schoolhouse door to greet the teacher. Out popped Nyarai, her smile still firmly intact.

There were sixty children ages three through six at the school, including a few children from Fairfield, but only two teachers. I made a mental note to tell my mom not to complain about the difficulties of keeping her twelve preschoolers in line when her assistant was absent for the day. That day and each following day, we sat in a semicircle, playing games, reading, and singing with the children. With Nyarai cuddled happily in my lap, we sang "Old McDonald" and "Jesus Loves Me." The children didn't understand a word of our English, but we all loved every minute of it. When it came time for a snack, all the children would scramble inside for warm milk and bread, pulling us along behind them.

Our last day at the crèche, Tiffany and I came with some toys and clothes we had stowed in our suitcases. The teacher called Nyarai over and told her that I had brought something for her. I pulled out a little pair of pink and white tennis shoes that had two straps of Velcro across the front. Nyarai and I attempted unsuccessfully for the next few minutes to get them to fit, but in the end it was futile. Her feet had already outgrown the sneakers. I stood up and watched as Nyarai left the bench and walked over to her younger friend, Sylvia. As one tear slid down her cheek, Nyarai brushed it away and placed the shoes on Sylvia's feet. They were a perfect fit. In that moment, Nyarai became my hero.

As the day was coming to a close, I held Nyarai's hand, as Moses took hold on my other side. Tiffany was behind us with her own two children in tow, and we began the long trek back to the orphanage. I looked over my left shoulder to see the beautiful African mountains and university far off in the distance, a feeling of contentedness washing over me that I had never felt before. After giving her a big hug, I gently set Nyarai down at the orphanage door and said good-bye one last time. She waved as I left and smiled her smile. I prayed that God would watch over her until He brought us back together. As I turned to leave, I wondered how her life would turn out. I wondered if I would be brave enough to return so I could know. At that moment, I didn't feel brave at all.

That night one of the women from our team who had traveled to Fairfield before explained that the children at the orphanage could be sponsored to help pay for their needs. I went early the next morning and talked to the matron at the hospital. This was the head nurse in charge of running the hospital when the doctor was away. Sitting behind the desk, wearing her green uniform with crisp white collar, she explained the details to me. I signed a paper eagerly and walked out of the room with a new sister, Nyarai. The matron promised to keep me informed about how she was doing and to send pictures when she could. I was very happy to have this connection with Nyarai, knowing it would help keep her memory from fading once I was an entire continent away.

Tiffany and I next passed through the baby room at the hospital. We had talked a lot over the last few days about our shared first reactions to the small baby Grace, who was HIV positive. Although we were still a little afraid, logically we knew it was unfounded. The best way to get over that fear was to do the very thing we were most afraid of, trusting that God would meet us there. Slipping gloves on, we both awaited our turn to hold Grace. Tiffany held her first, while my heart fought hard to find rest. Before I knew it, she was handing Grace to me.

As Tiffany went off to play with the other babies, I ducked into a side room with Grace tucked awkwardly between my stiffened arms. I began to sway her gently back and forth, my arms slowly relaxing to form around her. I sang to her quietly, "Amazing grace, how sweet the sound, / That saved a wretch like me. / I once was lost, but now am found, / Was blind but now I see." We were silent, then, as I continued to rock her back and forth, back and forth, in a slow clocklike rhythm. It was in that moment that I realized the meaning of the words I was singing, and God took hold of my heart and transformed it forever. Grace had AIDS, but suddenly there was nothing scary about her. She was only a tiny baby in need of as much love as I could offer her.

*   *   *   *   *

From that moment on, although I would always understand the fear that first registered in the eyes of other people when AIDS was mentioned, I would never again be afraid to hold, hug, touch, and love those who were HIV positive. God used Grace to take the fear away and replace it with something far more powerful: unconditional love that so overpowered fear that it completely wiped it away. I had no idea at that point how much that special love would be needed in the years to come. Looking back, though, I am sure I can sense God smiling in that moment as He watched His two little girls dancing together in that sparse hospital room as if nothing else in the world existed.

The rest of the trip was designated for touring Zimbabwe. We spent that weekend seeing beautiful waterfalls at Nyanga: the Mtarazi, Pungwe, and Nyangombe falls, and eating a gourmet lunch at the Montclair Hotel. As we ate our desserts and walked beside the crystal clear swimming pool, all of us started to feel bad. Hadn't we just left hungry, penniless people at Old Mutare? I could still see Nyarai running around the orphanage gate and into my arms, her mouth stained green from a Freeze-It (similar to a Popsicle). We decided to be grateful for this opportunity and enjoy it as much as possible.

That would not be difficult because the team was now headed for Hwange Safari Lodge. I was finally going to see the elephants I had dreamed of for so many years. My first opportunity came sooner than I thought it would. As Tiffany and I arrived in our beautiful hotel room, we looked out to a view of a watering hole complete with dozens of elephants. The scene was breathtaking until we discovered a notice on our window that read, "Please be advised that monkeys and baboons do enter the rooms." We were now living in a crazy paradise.

Before leaving the room, we practiced making hot tea, a custom that resulted from many years of British influence in Zimbabwe. The British had colonized Zimbabwe, which they named Rhodesia, in the late 1800s, but the country regained its independence in 1980. Tiffany noticed a different saying on the back of each sugar packet we used. Our favorite read, "You only live once, but if you work it right, once is enough." We decided this was going to be our new motto, knowing it would serve us well.

We quickly changed clothes and headed downstairs. The team was going for its first safari ride. We started down the dirt path, filling up three safari jeeps. I was enjoying the fresh air as we bumped along the road when suddenly Tiffany started pointing frantically to the left. I turned, and as my eyes refocused from the sunlight, I saw them: elephants began to appear right in front of us, coming through a mist of rays from the sun. They were so close we could hear every move of their trunks and stamp of their feet.

After a few moments, they disappeared into the trees just as suddenly as they had come.

We went on to see baboons crossing our path, the babies clinging to their mothers' bellies. The rest of the trip was a blur of zebras, wildebeests, and ostriches. We saw rhinos and a hippopotamus bathing in separate watering holes, with crocodiles basking in the sun nearby. A giraffe stooped to drink water, able to reach its long neck down only by splitting its thin legs wide. As time quickly disintegrated, the safari jeep headed back to the hotel, leaving the brilliant reds, oranges, and pinks of the African sunset slipping behind us through the flat tops of the acacia trees.

The next morning, we were up early for a second safari ride, and later in the afternoon, we flew on a tiny plane to Victoria Falls. An African had shown the falls, known then as the Smoke That Thunders, to Dr. David Livingstone in 1855 when he was traveling in Africa as a missionary and physician. He renamed the falls in honor of Queen Victoria.

From each of the lookouts, we could see a magnificent view, complete with miniature people rafting hundreds of feet below. We saw people bungee jumping from a bridge over the Zambezi River, which flowed rapidly beneath the falls. One of the lookouts had a permanent rainbow arched high over the river below.

Somehow by the end of the afternoon, Tiffany had convinced me to sign up for whitewater rafting the next morning. Now I was going to be one of those tiny rafters we had stared at from above. I became even more apprehensive when our leader said that our plane would be leaving only a few hours after our rafting excursion ended. We were informed that we would be getting on the plane, broken limbs or not.

By the next morning, Tiffany and I had collected our wet suits, helmets, and life jackets and were listening intently to the safety precautions given by our guide, who claimed he was "Captain Morgan." The most treacherous part of our journey was actually the descent to our rafts. We carefully began to slip down the slick paths and steep stairs that led to the water, clinging to the thin ropes that were at times the only thing keeping us upright. It took us a while to get situated in the boat, but after the first rapid, we loosened up a bit.

Conquering five more rapids and walking around a class six, attached on the side of a mountain by rope, we came to the last rapid of the day. Captain Morgan warned us that this rapid, which was named Gnashing Jaws of Death, was extremely dangerous. As we turned the corner, I wondered if it was too late to bail out, and I tightly gripped the sides of the raft. Instead of the deadly rapid we were expecting, there were only tiny little chops of waves that slightly resembled teeth, thus giving the "rapid" its name. So much for the gnashing jaws of death, but we were relieved. To complete our trip, we now had to ascend 750 very steep steps out of the gorge, clawing at times with both hands and feet to keep moving. I had never been so exhausted, and the Cokes that awaited us at the top had never tasted so good.

Now it was time to begin our journey home. After many hours of plane rides, we finally landed back in America. As we numbered off for the last time, we were definitely a closer group than the one that had started three weeks earlier. At only twenty years of age, I had completed my dream.

Before leaving for Africa, I had no idea what was in store, but I had learned valuable lessons and now had connections for the future as well as a new little sister. As I stepped off the bus and opened a bag of freshly baked cookies my mom had brought for me, I knew that a piece of my heart remained in Africa. Someday I would return and greet Nyarai on the long, dirt path winding through a most unique and special land. For now, however, there were cookies to be eaten and stories to be told.

Chapter 3

Change in Direction

*If you want to make God laugh, tell Him
your plans.*
—John Chancellor
As quoted from the *Los Angeles Times,*
June 13, 1996

After the novelty of the trip wore off, thoughts of Africa slowly began to fade. I had been given a brief sense of certainty when I was sitting in the orphanage, but taking steps of action proved much more difficult. The comforts of home were too easily distracting, and soon I managed to push any thoughts of returning far back in my mind until they were just wisps of memory. I finished my senior year of college and traveled to Charlotte, North Carolina, for what I thought was my dream job: teaching first grade. I was so excited to have a classroom of my own. Within the first few days of teaching, however, I realized I had made a big mistake. My children were wonderful, but something inside me knew I was not where I was supposed to be.

By October I was miserable and didn't know what to do. I scheduled an appointment with my pastor, and as soon as I entered his office and sat down, he leaned over the arm of his chair and with a knowing look said, "So, when did you first realize your calling?"

For a second, I had no idea what he was talking about, but an instant later, a memory floated back that I had buried deep inside me. It was the day I had sat in the orphanage courtyard with Moses and Nyarai and watched them share their mint. I had sensed so strongly at that moment that the Lord wanted me to live there someday with these children. Now years later, looking down at the carpet in my pastor's office, I suddenly became aware of how fully I had blocked that memory from my mind.

God had placed a call on my life; I just didn't know at the time what a calling was, so it had been easy to push those memories aside and believe I had been mistaken. What I experienced in the orphanage had cemented the truth about what God wanted to do through me. My response had been to develop temporary amnesia, because I knew what it meant. It meant leaving family, friends, possibly the chance of marriage, a good job, and all the comforts and famil-iarity of my own culture. At the time, I had not been willing to give up what seemed like everything. Yet, with one question, my pastor unknowingly brought it all back to the surface.

I explained all this in fragmented phrases, as my pastor listened calmly. When I finally came to the end of a thought, he asked if I would consider moving to Africa full-time. I laughed nervously. My pastor looked at me with a smile in his eyes and said, "Janine, not many people want to do what you are describing. God has placed other desires on their hearts. When people are filled with joy in doing something most others don't want to do, that usually means it is a calling from God. He has put that joy and that vision inside you." As I processed his words, it suddenly all made sense. In that moment, every-thing solidified for me, and I could think of nothing else I would rather do.

"I think you need to go to seminary," my pastor was saying, jarring me quickly back into reality. "I'm going to get you information about the school I attended in Kentucky."

"Seminary?" I asked with a hint of dismay. Perhaps this man had not been listening at all. I did not want to be a preacher, and seminary was for preachers. I was terrified of public speaking. I thought we had just agreed I should go to Africa and work with children.

However, my pastor explained that each one of us can be in ministry, but we are all called to minister in different ways. Seminary was for all who wanted a deeper relationship with God so they could devote their life's work to His purposes. My pastor explained that some people spent their lives doing what I was describing. They were called missionaries.

Shortly after our meeting, I took a day off from teaching and wrestled with this huge decision. I knew until I had dealt with it, it was not going away. On the one hand, I could stay right where I was and be provided for and comfortable. I realized I would always have that choice. I could always return to this safety, but now there was another option: one that was unknown and scary, but one that could be a great adventure I could not even imagine as I sat on the floor of my bedroom in my little apartment.

I started reading through Genesis in the Bible and identified immediately with Jacob as he wrestled with God through the night. My soul was literally wrestling with these two choices within me. I knew what God wanted, but I had to make His will my own. Finally, my mind exhausted from going back and forth, I surrendered. By the end of that day, I had made a very big decision, but I knew I could trust it. I could sense God was with me, urging me to be brave. I stood up from the floor at the end of the day with a certain assuredness that had not been there before. I would leave the safety of my teaching job and take the first step into the unknown.

The next few weeks were a whirlwind as I began looking around at different seminaries, amazed that I was even contemplating going. It turned out that the seminary my pastor had attended was one of the only schools in the country that offered a specific program in missions. The idea began to make more sense, as I realized I was not ready to go to Africa right away. I needed to be prepared, and I needed to have a stronger relationship with God.

Some of my friends and family were not quite so sure of my decision at first. Many had the same reaction to hearing the word *seminary* that I did when it was first mentioned. The word carried stigma and misunderstanding. But slowly my family and friends came to accept and support the decision I had made.

My mom and dad had always taught me and my brother to finish what we started, and I was only two months into my first year of teaching. The year would need to be completed before I could move forward with my plans. My first-grade students were learning to count by placing one number up each day we were in school. Some days it felt like day 180 would never come, ending the school year. Sitting at my desk with my assistant on the last day while the children watched a movie, I realized how precious they now were to me and how much they had grown. It had been difficult to stay, knowing what was ahead. With the last bell, I went home and began packing my bags in anticipation of the move.

*　　　*　　　*　　　*　　　*

Arriving in the tiny town of Wilmore, where two schools made up the majority of the population, I didn't know a single person there, except my new roommate. The very first day of orientation that fall, I met Reed, who would become my best friend. She had also been to Africa before. As the school year continued, Reed and I started talking about returning to Africa together the following summer. She wanted to go back to Ghana, where she had previously been. I was prepared to go with her to experience another part of Africa. As we made plans, however, I started feeling very strongly that I was to return to Zimbabwe. This meant going alone, but something in me knew I was supposed to go back to Fairfield Orphanage.

I found out through one of my professors that a girl named Nicole, who was about my age and from California, had been living at Old Mutare Mission for the past two years. We began writing back and forth, which helped to calm my fears. There had been bad reports from the press concerning Zimbabwe since I left four years earlier. The U.S. government had a constant travel warning issued advising U.S. citizens to travel to Zimbabwe only if absolutely necessary. There was a very definite reason for this warning.

The Zimbabwean government had begun a land-redistribution program right around the time Tiffany and I had first traveled there in 1998. When the British came to colonize the land in the late 1800s, they began farming the ring of land forming the country's borders, which had rich soil. This left the Zimbabweans with the middle part of the country, which was not fertile.

The British continued to make a good living farming the land even after Zimbabwe regained its independence in 1980. In the last four years, however, white Zimbabwean farmers had been forced off their farms by the government. The farmers were given no compensation for their homes, farm equipment, or land as their property was seized. These farmers were the descendants of the first colonizers and had been citizens of Zimbabwe for many generations. Some decided to leave the country, trying to avoid conflict, but others, who had purchased their land generations after the first colonizers came, stayed to protect what they felt belonged to them.

Once seized, the farmland was divided into small sections and given to Zimbabweans who had fought in the war of independence. This caused great food shortages over the next years, as the smaller pieces of land could not produce enough food to support the population, let alone have any left for export. Zimbabwe, which had formerly been known as the "breadbasket of southern Africa," quickly became a nation unable to feed its own people.

Hearing Nicole's stories, however, made life in Zimbabwe seem peaceful and inviting. She made the people come alive through her encounters with the children at the orphanage and tied in the lessons God was teaching her through each of them. I knew by reading Nicole's stories that I was not the only one who had been deeply changed by being around these children. There was something special about the children of Fairfield Orphanage that was easily evident. Nicole taught me through her e-mails to always look for what God wanted others to hear about the children of Zimbabwe. These children had a story to tell. It was up to us to tell it.

In April 2002, I received the following e-mail from Nicole:

> One warm day in February, I had only a few minutes for lunch, so I grabbed a

hunk of bread and cheese and headed up to the orphanage, where I knew the kids were expecting me. Now, I have long ago learned that there are two ways to bring food to the kids: you either have forty pieces or you have none. Knowing this, I worked fervently to stuff my chipmunk cheeks before I rounded the bend in the footpath. I was, of course, instantly spotted by one of my favorite little girls, Sylvia. After a ceremonious bear-hug greeting, there was no hiding my little treats. I broke the chunk of cheese in two, gave her one, and popped the other into my mouth. She looked curiously at the mysterious white blob, looked back at me, and promptly ran away. I was shocked. I thought, "Well, there's gratitude for you!"

I followed her up the path and saw her hiding behind a three-foot cement wall, protecting her prize from the other hungry mouths. I slid around the opposite side of the wall unseen, as one of the staff women came carrying bundles of laundry. She saw the little girl hiding and suspiciously asked, "Hey, what are you eating?"

"Um . . . don't know . . ."

"What? What do you mean you don't know? Why do you put this thing in your mouth that you don't know?"

"Niko gave it to me."

The woman smiled, seeing me listening from the other side of the wall. She teasingly asked, "Hmmm . . . what if Niko gave you a *snake*"?

Sylvia looked indignant and said, "Niko not give me a snake! Niko loves me!"

At this point, I slid down the wall, unnoticed, with tears in my eyes.

"Which of you, if his son asks for bread, will give him a stone? Or if he asks for a fish, will give him a snake? If you then, though you are evil, know how to give good gifts to your children, how much more will your Father in heaven give good gifts to those who ask him?" (Matt. 7:9–11).

This verse has meant a lot to me in times of frustration or disappointment, a reminder that God always gives me what I need or better, but never worse. Now this verse takes on new meaning for me as I work with some of the greatest kids I have ever known. They have one to ask for bread or fish. All they have is stones. They come to us abused, abandoned, or orphaned and have a hard time putting much trust in anyone. If a child can't even begin to fathom reliable, sincere human love, how much more inconceivable is God's love and sacrifice? My job is in wiping tears, holding hands, and lots of hugs.

I just returned to Zimbabwe last week after a month spent fund-raising for our building project. Arriving back at the mission, I was bombarded by hugs around my waist, kids climbing on my back, and a few attached to my knees. There, amongst all the chaos, was Sylvia, quiet, unmoving, with her eyes glued to me. She had this huge irrepressible smile on her face that said, "I just knew you would come back."

I love this job.

Niko

As I read this first e-mail from Nicole, tears streamed down my face. This was the same Sylvia that Nyarai had given her shoes to four years earlier. I had to wonder if Nyarai might also still be at the orphanage. Fairfield had started out as a baby orphanage that kept children only to the age of five, but Nicole was writing about Sylvia, who would have already turned seven. I could only pray that Nyarai would still be there when I returned. After receiving countless e-mails to assure me that Zimbabwe was not the scary place I heard about on the news, I took a step of faith and purchased my plane ticket. There was no turning back now. It was time to return to Africa. I wanted my own stories to write.

Chapter 4

Growing Pains

I seek not my own will, but the will of him who sent me.

—John 5:30 RSV

As I prepared to return to Zimbabwe at the end of my first year of seminary, stress surrounded me. Final exams were taking place Monday through Wednesday, and my plane left only two days later. I was going to be gone for two whole months. It was the longest stretch of time I had ever been away from my family. The day before I was to leave, I still could not get everything to fit into my suitcases. Reed came over late one afternoon and patiently helped to repack my things. She reminded me that two months wasn't really that long out of a whole lifetime. If nothing else, she said, this trip would teach me to never take home for granted, but in my heart I knew this would not be the last time I packed for Zimbabwe.

Just before I went to bed, I felt a slight pain in my right ear. It was barely noticeable, but by the next morning it had grown into a lingering dull ache. I decided to see the local doctor and have it checked before driving to the airport.

Sitting quietly in the doctor's office, I listened as she explained that I had an acute ear infection and that I should have come in days before. At that moment, the stress from finals and the trip preparations exploded. As the nurse gave me one injection after another, I began to cry uncontrollably. The doctor calmly continued explaining how to take my medicines and said if there was any way I could postpone the trip, I should. She had been a missionary herself for many years in Africa and had a knowing smile on her face. Finally she said, "God will be with you if you decide to go, but you are going to be in a lot of pain." I watched helplessly as she walked out of the room.

I went back to my apartment in a panic. I did the only thing I knew to do: I called my mom. Through tears I explained what the doctor had said and that I didn't think I could get on the plane. I was too afraid. Wouldn't it be better for me to come home and reschedule a later flight date? I knew my mom, of all people, would understand. The words that came out of her mouth, however, were not anything that I would have ever expected. Looking back, I know they were not from her.

She calmly explained that I needed to get my luggage ready and go to the airport. She reminded me that I had felt a very strong call to go back to

Zimbabwe, even though there were many reasons why it would be safer not to go. If I could trust God to take care of me for two months there, I could trust Him to get me through the plane ride. She said she loved me and would be praying for me, and she hung up the phone.

Staring at the receiver that now had a steady dial tone, I could hardly believe what I had heard, but something in me knew she was right. I got up from the couch and washed my face, loaded my suitcases into the car, and headed for the airport. It was only much later that I realized how much faith my mom must have had to say those words.

I made it to London, clutching my Bible like a fanatic the whole way. I am sure the people on either side of me were worried that I was about to jump up and start preaching to everyone, but I didn't care. It gave me a tangible way to remember who was with me. Miraculously, I didn't have any problems with my ears during those first two flights. My joy was quickly overclouded, however, as all the medicines began to take effect. I had no appetite and had not had anything to drink in many hours, causing dehydration. I boarded the plane for Zimbabwe and moved all the way to my window seat at the back, next to a large Zimbabwean man dressed in a business suit.

By the middle of the ten-hour flight, I began to feel dizzy and nauseous. The chair in front of me began to spin, and I suddenly took a flying leap over the unfortunate man in the aisle seat, trying to make it to the tiny bathroom. I spent the remainder of the flight curled up in my small seat, my head, still spinning, pressed against the window. Two thoughts continued to float through my head. They were my mom's two steadfast pieces of advice: "This too shall pass," and "Everything happens for a reason." At that moment, I could not see the reason for the miserable state I was in, but I had come this far. I would not turn back now.

Arriving safely at the Harare airport, I slept most of the three-hour drive to Old Mutare Mission. I started feeling more like myself as the driver pulled onto the main dirt road of the mission, and I began recognizing familiar sights from my first trip. Finally I arrived at the little house just next door to the orphanage, where I would be staying with Nicole, her brother who was visiting, and Cecilia, a Zimbabwean who worked at the orphanage.

I stepped through the front door and into the coolness of the square cement house. The floors were made of dark red clay, and the sun shone through the open windows as a breeze filtered in, blowing the green cloth curtains. There on a simple wooden table sat a cold Mazoe orange drink, which was offered to me by the one and only Nicole. As she stood tall to greet me, I wondered what it would be like to live for the next two months in a strange place with people I had never met. Everything felt foreign, and I knew only God could make it familiar.

The next day, Nicole took me to the same maternity wing I had visited on my previous trip, the place where the orphaned babies were kept. Although the faces had obviously changed over four years, the conditions were still the same. The babies lay alone in cribs all day long for the first year of their lives before being moved to the orphanage. Nurses came in every few hours to check on them in between caring for sick patients. The babies all had flattened spots on the backs of their heads where the hair had rubbed off from the babies' lying in the same position for so many hours a day. Many were having problems developmentally and could not sit or stand at the proper age. My little Grace had long since passed away, and now lined up in a straight row in front of me were my new friends: Tapiwa, Gift, Tariro, Panashe, Tendai, and Jayne.

As we began to walk to the orphanage, Nicole told me about a lot of changes that were taking place. For years Fairfield Orphanage had been under the hospital's domain. Different staff rotated in every eight hours to care for the forty-two orphans living in the rundown building. It was meant to be an orphanage for babies up to the age of five, but social welfare was so backed up that they had nowhere else to send the children. No one had come to pick up any of the older children for many years. The oldest child was now nine years of age, and the small rusted cribs were forced to hold two to three children every night. The one small house was no longer sufficient for the growing boys and girls.

During the day, the children pulled bricks from the walls and played with them, along with old broken chairs. Children licked the walls and ate dirt, their bodies searching for missing nutrients anywhere they could be found. The smiles I could begin to see through the broken windowpanes, however, did not seem to reflect the lack of material possessions.

Nicole was working with a group of individuals from the States known as FOSA, Fairfield Orphanage Sponsorship Association, and they were raising funds to build twelve houses for the children. Each home would have a "mother" and "auntie" hired to take care of ten children, who would become "brothers" and "sisters" to one another. The mothers would receive special training and be with the children twenty-four hours a day. The aunties would consist of the old staff from the orphanage. They would continue living with their own families and work at the new Fairfield Children's Homes during the day. After the homes were completed, they would be able to keep the children from birth to eighteen years of age. The children would not have to be moved from one orphanage to another, but would now be members of a surrogate family.

As we stepped into the orphanage, I asked the question for which I had been nervously awaiting an answer: "Do you know of a girl named Nyarai?"

"Yeah," Nicole answered immediately. "She is now our oldest child at Fairfield."

Within a few minutes, Nyarai stood before me, her beautiful dark eyes still sparkling. As I watched her, I could see she had turned into a responsible and helpful girl during the years I had been away. Being the oldest girl, she had a lot of cooking and cleaning tasks, which she carried out quietly with a smile on her face. As I grew to know Nyarai better over the next two months, I would learn that behind the smile was a lot of mischief as well. For now, I was just glad to see her again.

I took Nyarai to see the playground being built by Nicole's brother and to see the foundations of the first houses. I explained that soon she would live in one of those houses. As we talked, I told Nyarai that she had been my special sister for the last four years and that I had come back to see her. She would be ten years old in two months and wanted a doll for her birthday. I could not believe that she was here with me again, now old enough for us to be friends. That day the love I felt for this little girl grew even stronger.

Those first few days, as I took in my surroundings, I went to the nursery every day, taking the babies out of their cribs and playing with them on the floor. I laid the children on their stomachs to begin strengthening their neck muscles and helped them practice sitting up. Some of the children were old enough to learn to walk, but their leg muscles had not developed enough. With the help of some of the nurses, we began moving the babies' legs each day, hoping they would become limber and strong.

Each evening, as I began to settle into a routine on the mission, I had the chance to know my Zimbabwean roommate, Cecilia, better. By the light of the fire each night, Nicole and I would play cards, along with her brother and another girl, Emily, who was also visiting from America. Cecilia would sit sewing her baby blankets to sell, and as she worked, she would teach me new Shona words.

Cecilia also had many laughs watching my first attempt at washing my clothes by hand in the bathtub. I routinely turned most things pink. After a good scrub, my socks would remain slightly tinged brown from the dirt, although when Cecilia put her hands to them, they seemed to come out whiter than when I first bought them. It was going to take a lot of practice, but there was no washing machine to rely on, so the process would need to be mastered.

As I got used to the mission, Nicole also familiarized me with the nearby town of Mutare, about a fifteen-minute drive from the mission, up and over a massive mountain known as Christmas Pass. The exchange rate for money had jumped over the last four years from Zim$28 for US$1, and a person could now get over Zim$350 dollars for every US$1. By the time I left two months later, the rate would be close to six hundred to one.

Almost every time we went to town, the rates had moved higher. The same woman who sat clanking change in a bowl on the side of the street in 1998 was now more silent, needing to collect an ever-increasing number of paper bills in order to have enough money to buy food. All day long she sat on the sidewalk, repeating over and over again in a loud voice, *"Ndinokumbirawo rubatsiro?"* which means, "Please, may you help me?"

That night I woke up in total darkness and was unable to get back to sleep. This would be the first of many sleepless nights I spent in Africa over the following years. Part of me began to realize with finality that Zimbabwe was going to be a bigger part of my life than just these few months. I could still hear the haunting words of the woman from the street as she repeated, *"Ndinokumbirawo rubatsiro?"* I envisioned each of the children at the orphanage tucked closely together in their cots, fast asleep.

That night I had to turn everything over to God and tell Him, "I will go anywhere for You and do anything You want me to do. Just promise to stay with me." It was scary and very real saying this while staring at a blank wall in Africa far from the comforts of home. After listening for Nicole's steady breathing from the other side of the room and making sure that she was asleep, I turned back toward the wall and let the tears fall freely until sleep came.

Later that week, Nicole, Emily, and I were in charge of the children for a few days while the mothers who had been hired for the new homes, along with the current staff, were being trained. The mothers had been chosen through the mission church before I came and were mostly widows with older children or women who had no children of their own. This would ensure that they grew close to their new family of ten orphans.

After the first few days of training, they were put in charge of the children for one morning to see how they could handle them. Nicole went up after about an hour to check on them and came back with a shocked look on her face. She said the front room was clean and for the first time did not have the distinctive smell of urine we had all become so used to. The children were all nicely dressed and sitting in rows, quietly eating a snack.

This was a huge improvement from the old methods. One of the staff usually dumped a large box of clothes on the ground each morning, and the children would rummage for something that would fit. They would then roam around, infants often left unattended on blankets while the other children threw things at one another. I began to see why the new children's homes were so important. Each mother was now taking responsibility for her own group of children, showing the older ones how to assist their younger brothers and sisters. The transformation in the children's behavior was immediate and truly incredible.

A doctor came to check on the babies the next day and told us that the president had just declared a state of emergency for the AIDS epidemic. This meant that drugs could now be given at cheaper costs to ensure everyone could receive them. The drugs, known as ARVs, helped boost the immune system and ensured that the afflicted individuals were able to live longer. Nicole decided that all the children should be tested the following week so they could be started on the drugs if found positive.

On the first day of testing, we decided to start with the babies and toddlers. By the time the older children had heard the screams and seen the taped arms of the toddlers, they were all a little apprehensive about going with us. Each of the older children was allowed to choose one person to go in with them while their blood was drawn. Nyarai looked over all her choices and picked me. I understood the sacrifices of coming to Zimbabwe, but in that moment, I realized how much more I had gained.

The results came back a few days later. Miraculously, for a country where the AIDS epidemic was quickly sweeping its way across the land, none of the forty-two children at Fairfield were HIV positive. A few days later, however, a small boy named Learnmore was found in a paper sack left sitting on one of the hospital benches. As the patients were all clearing out for the day, one of the women had noticed the bag and looked inside. Learnmore was extremely malnourished and weak, so he hadn't even moved to let anyone know he was there. Immediately the nurses admitted him, and after his health stabilized, he was transferred to the orphanage. After testing him, we discovered that Learnmore was HIV positive, and he had tuberculosis as well. Emily took the little boy as her own and began visiting him daily.

Within days, we had a second new child. As I was leaving the maternity wing one evening after visiting the babies, a frail, thin man walked in, carrying something wrapped tightly in a blanket. He looked at me and said something in Shona before handing the bundle into my arms and turning to walk away. Inside was a tiny baby. I looked at her for a few moments and then gazed down the long, dark hallway, wondering what I was supposed to do. The entire length of the baby's body fit between the tips of my fingers and my elbow. She looked like she needed to be placed in an incubator.

A nurse came through a few minutes later and explained that the baby's name was Beatrice. Her mother had just passed away, and the father was in shock. He had left the baby here so he could get the necessary papers from social welfare to leave the child with us. He could not handle taking care of the baby alone.

As I looked down at tiny Beatrice that first night, her miniature fingers wrapping around mine, I fell in love with the new baby girl. Over the next weeks, I continued to visit Beatrice in the maternity wing, but her health never seemed to improve. She was not gaining weight, and it was suspected that, like Learnmore, she was HIV positive. She was so tiny that no one wanted to take a blood sample to find out for sure.

One night shortly after Beatrice arrived, I walked toward the maternity wing to check on her and the other babies, feeling the crisp night air against my bare arms. I suddenly had a sense that I should stay until the houses were completed in December, instead of leaving at my original departure time in July. By then the children would be well cared for by their new mothers, but for now they needed people to consistently love them. As I entered the maternity wing, however, my thoughts were quickly placed on hold.

As I changed three-month-old Tendai into his nightclothes, laying him gently back into his crib, I noticed he did not look well. I knew even minor illnesses were dangerous to the babies, as the over-worked staff fought to keep up with all their obli-gations. Nicole had explained how three babies had died within the last six months in the same hospital room where Tendai now cried out in pain from his crib. Something that could easily be taken care of with a dose of antibiotics could grow to more serious problems if overlooked. I spoke to the head nurse, and after checking him, she placed him on an IV.

Over the next days, Tendai did not seem to improve. The only medicines available for small children at the mission hospital were a few bottles of over-the-counter syrups. Even with more attention given to Tendai's condition, it did not look encouraging. Every time I tried to feed him, he could not keep anything in his stomach.

As I entered the room the fourth day, Tendai was whimpering in pain, and his breath was short. His eyes were two wide disks of fear staring out from between the slats of his crib. I had no idea what could make a three-month-old child look so afraid.

When I asked the nurse what she thought was wrong with him, her answer shocked me. From the medication and sickness, Tendai had become severely dehydrated. As she spoke, my mind flashed back to a little over a month before when I was curled into my airplane seat, weak from dehydration and all alone. I knew that all I had wanted was to know that someone was with me and that everything would be okay. Looking down at Tendai, I knew I had nothing to offer him medically, but I could help him know that he was not alone. After hours of holding him, the nurse told me there was nothing else we could do.

As she started to walk away, I begged her to take him to the main hospital in town. They had more tests and medicines available. The nurse seemed to struggle internally. She finally sent me to the matron, who explained that Tendai did not have a sponsor, and the orphanage had no funding for medical care in town. The mission hospital had always provided basic care free of charge to the children at Fairfield. As she spoke, I realized the magic words—*I'll pay*—and spoke them quickly.

Tendai was rushed immediately to Mutare General Hospital, and my mind raced with thoughts of emptying bank accounts and pleading for financial assistance from home. I went into shock, realizing I had just promised to pay a hospital bill without having any idea of what the cost would be. Over the next few hours in town, Tendai was X-rayed, examined, and placed on several different types of medicine.

While Nicole and I waited for Tendai's doctor in the children's ward, we noticed a small girl in the corner. Her clothes stretched at least half a foot past her legs, and over them she wore a tattered terry-cloth woman's robe. The nurses told us her name was Tsitsi, meaning "sympathy" or "compassion." They explained that her parents had died, and her aunt had abandoned her at the hospital six months ago. Social welfare had not yet placed the young girl at an orphanage. Instead, she had become a fixture in the children's ward, wandering around each day with no one to look after her.

Throughout the evening, we noticed the mothers of the other children intentionally ignoring Tsitsi. She appeared sickly, and no one seemed to want to take on the responsibility for her care. When she began to cry, I picked her up and rocked her. I heard the women whispering to one another and could feel their stares. Tsitsi collapsed against me and held tight. The women began saying things to her and laughing. Only later did I find out they were taunting the little girl: "Who is holding you? You don't even know her name."

Luckily, Nicole had become proficient at translating Shona after a year working in Zimbabwe. She was also very good at pulling off an oblivious American look so that no one caught on to her ability to understand what was being said. The very next day, Nicole went straight to the social-welfare office and petitioned for Tsitsi to be released to Fairfield Orphanage. After much insistence, she convinced them that we would not leave Tsitsi in the hospital, and four days later, they agreed to let us take her to Fairfield.

During those four days, Tendai's bright smile began to return. The kind pediatrician who had been assigned to Tendai's case said I could take him home that same day. As we gathered his things and prepared to leave, the doctor told us that he was glad Tendai had come when he did, because he would not have made it through another night without the right medications.

With both children in tow, we went to check out of the hospital. I received the bill, which totaled Zim\$530. I stared at it in amazement for a few moments before pulling out a few bills from my pocket and pushing it over to the man behind the counter. In that moment, my whole world stopped making sense. Zim\$530 equaled approximately ninety cents in U.S. money. My baby had almost died over pocket change. We took both Tendai and Tsitsi home that night, grateful that they were both happy and healthy.

A few weeks later, it was time for me to go home on my scheduled July flight. I had decided to return to Zimbabwe a few weeks later with everything I needed to stay for the remainder of the year. I was happy to be going home, but I also knew I definitely needed to come back. That voice inside that had urged me to stay was still there. All I needed as a reminder was to think of Learnmore laughing at the other children as they played, or being able to hold baby Beatrice in my arms, or seeing Nyarai's smile. It was enough to think of Tendai and Tsitsi happily home from the hospital. For now, though, I felt tired and ready for the break.

Within a few days, I was dumped back into American life after the long plane rides home. The last thing I wanted to think about was getting back on the plane to return in just a few weeks. I returned to my apartment to find my roommate waiting up for me. Although I hadn't slept in almost two days, we stayed up most of the night as she generously listened to my stories. I felt disconnected, knowing that I would not be home for long. I had within me a conviction to return to Africa. I now felt assurance that this was the place God had called me to.

Chapter 5

Lessons in Obedience

Never doubt in the dark what God told you
in the light.
—V. Raymond Edman
As quoted from Rick Warren's
Purpose Driven Life

For the next few days, I reveled in American life. I hung out with friends, ate fast food, and wandered around Wal-Mart for hours, just looking at the newness of everything and the thousands of different kinds of toothpaste. I felt like an outsider. The ease of living in America overcame me almost immediately, however, and the thought of going back to Zimbabwe suddenly seemed so hard.

At first my children ran through my mind all the time: baby Beatrice, Tendai, Nyarai. Only a few days earlier, I had hugged Cecilia good-bye, saying I was coming right back. But sitting in my comfortable apartment and being able to watch television and talk to my friends and family anytime that I wanted quickly began to cloud my conviction to return. I began to convince myself and everyone around me of all the reasons I should not go back to Zimbabwe.

I turned out to be very successful at it. The plane ticket was too expensive, I reasoned. Furthermore, if I went back now, I would have to graduate a semester later, delaying any full-time work I could do overseas. My family and friends had gone to a lot of trouble to set everything up for me to stay in Zimbabwe through December, but now I was reversing everything in a desperate attempt to stay home.

After making up my mind, steadily ignoring that voice within that had urged me to stay in Zimbabwe, I wrote to Nicole, elaborately explaining why I would not be returning. She responded with her usual wit, but underlying her humor I knew I had just disappointed many people. More damaging, I had just disappointed the children to whom I had promised to return. I had disappointed myself. Something had hardened my heart, and I stubbornly refused to get back on the plane.

During my absence, Nicole continued to send updates. My heart ached each time I heard from her, and I mourned the decision I had made. Emily had decided to stay in Zimbabwe for the semester and brought Learnmore to live with them in our house because he had become very ill. Nicole became very close to Tsitsi. She did not adjust well at the orphanage, and Nicole ended up taking her to live with them as well. They now had a house full. Tsitsi changed almost immediately from the distant child we had first met at the hospital who flew into fits of screaming and crying anytime she didn't get her way. Nicole discovered that Tsitsi was smart, funny, and affectionate, and the two instantly bonded as mother and daughter. Nicole was even considering adoption.

In one e-mail, Nicole mentioned in passing that chicken pox was spreading through the orphanage, joking that we should invest in calamine stock. But within a week, it was clear the situation was nothing to laugh about. I received an e-mail that sent me into a steady downward spiral into depression. I knew we had to trust God, even if it didn't make sense to us at the time, but I didn't know how many more letters like this one I could handle or how many more Nicole would be able to write. Little did I know then that God was preparing me to deal with a situation that would be repeated more times than I cared to count during my life in Zimbabwe.

Nicole, August 2002

Sunday night I waited and waited for my family to call. I was tired from a long day of hand washing laundry, sweeping, scrubbing floors on my knees, cooking porridge, and playing nurse to my sick little chicken pox girl. For the last month, little four-and-a-half-year-old Tsitsi has been staying with me, and I have had the inexplicable joy of being a full-time parent. I have spent much time deliberating the pros and cons of adoption and what it would mean to become a single, twenty-five-year-old parent. After just a few weeks of having Tsitsi around the house, I was sure I was ready to make the lifetime commitment to this little girl who had totally stolen my heart.

Tsitsi is the most precious little girl I have ever known. She knows all of the right manners, is charming and funny, and downright hilarious at times. She is very self-disciplined and rarely misbehaves. She only cries when she is tired or when she is afraid of the dark. She has this thing about mirrors. Whenever we walk into a restaurant bathroom or pass a plate-glass window she shouts, "Niko, look!"

I always ask, "What do you see there?" and she always answers, "Tsitsi neNiko" (Tsitsi and Niko) then throws her arms around my neck and kisses my cheek.

When she starts to get tired, she likes to curl up in a ball in my lap and tries to sleep in the crook of my arm. From this awkward position, she reaches up her little hand and points out one finger. She waits patiently while I pretend not to notice. When the little finger finally "surprises" me, I give her a baby kiss on the tip of that finger, which brings out a huge smile and an instant withdrawal of the hand. She holds the finger very close to her face and examines it intensely, looking for some trace or mark. She doesn't understand when I tell her in English that there are no tangible proofs of love: you just know when it is there.

Tsitsi hardly slept Sunday night as most of her big blisters started to pop and break, and she tried and tried to get comfortable. Early that morning I gave her a bath and rubbed her down with calamine lotion, and she finally fell asleep. She refused to eat her lunch and would barely take any liquids that day. Although it had been more than a week of chicken pox, more spots kept appearing, and I was beginning to get worried.

On Saturday we had started a five-day penicillin injection series that helps the body fight complications and skin infections. After lunch I took her to the mission hospital for her third injection and asked to talk to the doctor. He sat me down and explained that Tsitsi had just been diagnosed as HIV positive. As I bit my lip and choked back the tears, he prescribed an extra course of antibiotics and fever reducers, as well as ointment for the sores that had developed inside her mouth and tongue. It was going to be a rough course ahead of us.

That night I stayed up until half past four, reading medical journals, administering Tsitsi's medicines, cleaning her sores, and bathing her as often as she would let me. More and more pox kept appearing, and at one count, she had more than twenty-five just on the palm of one tiny hand. Her fever was steady at 102 degrees, and the medicines and bathing did little to calm it.

The next morning, she was admitted to the hospital, with a third course of antibiotics. Her fever peaked at 104.3 before it finally started coming down. My healthy, happy little girl had quickly deteriorated into a state of confusion and suffering.

That afternoon we took her back to the house. There was nothing more the hospital could do for her, and since her fever had come down, she was again playful, and her appetite returned. She ate dinner, drank several cups of water, and took her medicines willingly. She climbed on my lap and played with my fingers again. I didn't know it then, but it was the beginning of the end—our last chance to say good-bye.

Within a few minutes, she began violently vomiting and complaining that she felt cold. She was extremely disoriented, unable to walk properly, and her temperature dropped to 96.1. I wrapped her in her favorite white blanket and started running toward the hospital. Emily and Cecilia were close behind as I reached the front doors. Nurses phoned the doctor, who came running as well. The last thirty minutes were terrible: delusions, screaming, and seizures. The staff tried everything they possibly could. I held her hand, she looked me in the eyes, and then she was gone.

The entire day before, she had been waking up complaining of being tired and saying, "Niko, I'd like to sleep, please." I'd lay her head in my lap and tell her to close her eyes, but I think the sleep she needed was deeper. She needed more peace than I could offer her. I am comforted that her suffering is over.

The hardest part is how fast everything happened. Last week Emily and I sat playing with her, talking about what she would be like as a teenager and how well she would adapt to living in the States. In forty-eight hours, I went from thinking about which university she might attend to picking out an outfit for her to be buried in.

Next week, once we get the paperwork from social welfare, I will bury my little girl. There is no punishment, no torture, ever invented that could compare to this. I cannot imagine the pain of millions of families in Africa going through the same situation, most of whom don't have resources to offer pain-killers and antibiotics to their little ones.

AIDS is an unmerciful thief, and no family in Zimbabwe goes untouched. In the few months that Tsitsi stayed with us, she was a light and inspiration in this community, which loved her very much. I cannot possibly express how much I will miss her or how much she meant in my life.

Tsitsi had been taken into our home, cared for, and loved until her death. She died in the arms of her new mother, Nicole. She spent her last days with people who loved her, instead of wandering aimlessly around the hospital room where we had found her. As I read Nicole's message, I couldn't help but remember that we had found Tsitsi in the first place only because of Tendai's sickness. He had suffered temporarily, but possibly for a greater good.

Now I was back in school, and the bad news continued to hit me. The next message I received from Nicole stated that Learnmore had passed away, also after contracting chicken pox. The immune systems of the HIV-positive children could not support chicken pox coursing through their bodies. Emily's mother flew all the way from the States to be with her for the funeral. Learnmore's precious smile had captured them all, and he had truly lived up to his name, teaching them many beautiful lessons during the short time he lived with them. Tsitsi and Learnmore were buried side by side in the mission cemetery at the top of the hill behind the high school. Both had plaques with the Fairfield logo and quotes chosen by their mothers, Nicole and Emily.

On October 15, I received another e-mail from Nicole, stating that baby Beatrice had passed away as well. She suffered from "failure to thrive," a term used for HIV- positive children who did not gain weight. Social welfare would not only have to notify

Beatrice's father of her death but would also have to alert him to the fact that he was most likely HIV positive as well.

Beatrice had been my baby. Her father had handed her over to me. Tsitsi had Nicole at her side. Learnmore had Emily to comfort him when he was in pain. Who was there to rock Beatrice to sleep and speak up on her behalf when she was so desperately ill? It should have been me. The comforts from home could no longer curb the suffering and guilt raging inside me.

Although the news of these deaths was difficult for me to handle at home, they weighed even more heavily on Emily and Nicole, who experienced them firsthand. By November they began preparing to leave the country. I continued to fight depression throughout that semester and into December. Then, almost as instantly as it had appeared, it lifted sometime in January. I was free again. If I had stayed in Zimbabwe as I had originally felt I was supposed to do, this was the time when I would have returned to school. The exactness of the timing did not escape my attention.

I once again felt a longing to see my children in Zimbabwe be given a chance at life. There were now forty-two specific faces among the millions who would remain forever in my prayers and three tiny angels whose memories needed to live on. God would once again fill me with a fierce determination to return to my children in Zimbabwe, overcoming the months of sorrow that had preceded.

One of our professors challenged us at the beginning of that semester with a quote from Frederick Buechner: "The place God calls you to is the place where your deepest gladness and the world's deep hunger meet." I instantly knew my answer. I had been given a second chance, and this time I would not back down.

The following September, in 2003, I received a letter from Nicole, who had returned to Zimbabwe for a short time to see how everything was progressing with the building of the new homes, which were now extremely behind schedule. She wrote excitedly to Emily and me, informing us of the new developments. There were now two mothers in the maternity wing, always available to feed and bathe the babies, change their nappies (diapers), and attend to them when they cried. All the children at the orphanage were wearing clean clothes, noses wiped and no longer eating dirt or throwing stones at one another. We had never thought it was possible. With this positive update, I felt more determined than ever to return after graduation.

That November I began looking for mission agencies willing to send me to Zimbabwe. Every group I talked to gave me the same response: they would not send a single woman alone to Zimbabwe. Most agencies were actually pulling their missionaries out of Zimbabwe because of the volatile political situation and huge inflation rates.

One day I was in the check-out line at the grocery store when a friend walked up behind me. He asked how my search was going, and I lamented about mission agencies not willing to send single women. "We will," he replied. He handed me a card and exited the store. Looking down, I saw the logo *CornerStone International* at the top of the card. Back at my apartment, I set it on top of my dresser and passed by it over the next few weeks. Finally I gathered the courage to call and set up an appointment. It seemed like a last chance.

The next day I sat nervously in the front office with the director. There was a map of the world covering the entire wall to the left of me, and each time I felt I was about to lose my nerve, I fixed my eyes on the tiny circle of Zimbabwe. I talked to the director about what I felt called to do. I understood the dangers but felt that I was safer walking in God's will in Zimbabwe than being disobedient by living somewhere else.

The director explained that CornerStone was a group of people whose primary goal was to pray for the nations. They felt called to send people into the mission field, praying for them and the countries in which they served. As long as I felt a strong calling from God, they would trust Him and send me, even if I was alone.

Once I located a mission board, my decision was confirmed in little ways over the following semester before I graduated. One day I went into chapel to find a woman speaking about her experiences as a missionary. At the end, she seemed to look directly at me before stepping down from the podium and saying sternly, "Go, go, go!" Then she turned and walked off the stage. Each time I started to doubt, there was a letter in the mail from a friend in Zimbabwe or a face on television that looked just like one of my children. As I was driving home one day, I received a phone call from my mom. A couple from church felt led to use their tax return to pay for the entire cost of my plane ticket. After that confirmation, I began to make plans to return.

During the final senior chapel at school, we each went forward and laid items on the altar that represented our ministry. I brought a picture of my little boy Tendai, now over two years old, along with the Zimbabwean flag. Our chaplain anointed each of us with oil. With Reed standing beside me, I felt a power and boldness come over me. Together my friends and I prayed for one another during that final chapel. It had been the most amazing three years of my life up to that point. I had formed friendships that would last throughout the rest of my life.

As I turned to leave, however, someone came up to me and with fear and sorrow in her voice pleaded, "Don't go to Zimbabwe. It is just too dangerous."

"I have to go," I replied. "I know I am supposed to be there." After so many months of doubt and fear mixing in with my decisions, I now knew with certainty that it was time to walk forward with confidence into the light.

Chapter 6

Humble Beginnings

*If you do the unexpected, unexpected things
will happen.*

—Anonymous

I arrived back in Zimbabwe in June of 2004, just two weeks after graduating from seminary. It had been two years since I had been to Zimbabwe, and I knew a lot had changed. I felt God had called me to work with children in Old Mutare, so my only intent was to discover an area of need and see how I had been equipped to fill it. I returned to Old Mutare Mission to live with Cecilia, my old Zimbabwean roommate, who was now the assistant administrator of the new Fairfield Children's Homes.

Turning onto the long dirt road at the entrance of the mission, I saw the large white and gray walls of the mission church directly in front of me. Dust flew up behind the car as it veered left past the buildings that clustered together to form Hartzell Primary School. The cement slab where the high school students played volleyball and basketball topped a slight hill on the right, and the car slowed as a sea of children parted in front of me, walking slowly to have time to talk on their way to their next class. Before I reached the hospital, a new set of brick houses right along the road's edge caught my eye. "This must be my new home," I thought, smiling to myself.

Where a long, empty field had once stood, there were now twelve brand-new brick homes built in a circle around a playground, as well as a large hut structure that served as a conference room. The transition from Fairfield Orphanage to Fairfield Children's Homes was complete, the children having just moved into their new homes a few weeks before I arrived. The structure that had once served as Fairfield Orphanage now loomed empty at the top of the hill farther down the road, an eerie reminder of what used to be.

Directly in front of me, however, were homes where families lived, with over fifty orphans and twenty-five mothers and aunties to care for them. The children now lived in families of ten, being cared for by their own assigned mothers. The number of orphans at the children's homes was increasing daily, as social welfare produced more and more abandoned babies, happy that there was a safe haven to bring them to. Within a few months, Fairfield would come to have nearly eighty children under its care.

The children were still making their initial adjustments to family life. They were not used to living in such big houses with so few people, but everyone quickly adjusted. The mothers were diligent at forming bonds with their children, and they soon became a real family.

My first few weeks there were busy. I spent time getting reacquainted with the children and tutoring some of the older ones after school. I also attended morning devotions each day with the new staff. It was difficult to remember so many new names! I was put at ease right away, however, when I found Emily there, spending another month with the children. It was so good to see a familiar face, and the two of us had fun catching up as we lay side by side on our mats on the cement floor in the room we shared.

We had experienced plenty of time in Zimbabwe with no television, and both of us had learned from the past. This time our two laptop computers blazed long into the night as we watched episodes of *Friends* until we fell asleep. We didn't often get a full night's sleep, however, because of the new baby that we could hear crying constantly and the confused rooster that began crowing each morning before the sun was even thinking about rising.

After two weeks of adjusting to my new environment, Rumbidzai, a Zimbabwean friend whom I had met in America, invited me to go with her while she visited relatives. I stayed with her for two weeks, only later finding out how valuable that short time would be. I learned much about Shona culture from my time with Rumbidzai as she patiently explained different situations to me. This knowledge would help me immensely in the next months when I began to navigate with no other Americans around. I would be returning to a much quieter household, as Emily and others would be traveling back to the States, leaving me on my own.

I met Rumbidzai in Harare, the capital city. We spent the first few days with her husband's sister, affectionately known as "Tete," or Auntie. Tete had been given all the money from my savings account a few weeks before I arrived, and in return she presented me with my new form of transportation: a 1983 Mitsubishi Lancer. This was a true Zimbabwean car, and I fit right in on the road, the bright yellow exterior and leopard-print seat covers making me easy to spot. We traveled a few days later to her rural home, where we met both Rumbidzai's and her husband's family.

In Zimbabwe most families have a rural home where part of the family lives in huts, growing maize and vegetables and keeping animals. Other family members live in the cities, trying to find jobs to buy other necessities for the family. On this trip, my car tackled the dirt roads and potholes deftly. Once we arrived at Rumbidzai's rural home, I was instantly put to work.

We trekked through a small wooded area on a narrow dirt footpath that wound its way to a water pump in an open area. To work the pump, one woman would throw her weight on the pump handle, moving it up and down until water began pouring from the spout. The other woman would collect the water in buckets or jugs, changing them out when the water sloshed to the top. Both women would then lift the heavy buckets onto a folded cloth on top of their heads and move slowly back up the hill toward the huts. Everyone found it very amusing to watch me attempt to carry water in a bucket on my head. While Zimbabwean women could easily balance twenty liters without holding onto the buckets or spilling a single drop, I could barely manage my little five-liter bucket and ended up soaked from head to toe by the time I arrived back at the hut.

Later that night, we ate *sadza* cooked on an open fire in the middle of the kitchen hut. Each rural home usually contained a block cement building where the family slept, as well as a round hut with a thatched roof and clay walls that was used as a kitchen. Inside the kitchen hut, men and older boys sat on a smooth black slab of cement built into the wall, while the women and younger children sat on large straw mats on the ground.

On her knees, a young girl would go around to each person, pouring warm water over their hands and catching the water in a bowl she held underneath. This was the way hands were washed before a meal. Food was then served first to the men, usually by a daughter-in-law. The daughter-in-law (*muroora*) often did most of the work when she lived with or visited her husband's parents. Unfortunately for Rumbidzai's sister-in-law, she was the only one and had a lot of work to do while we visited.

That night I slept beside Rumbidzai on the only mattress in the house. Her entire family of women and younger children slept huddled close together all over the cement floor. Waking in the middle of the night, I crept through the maze of bodies and quietly stepped outside. There was a full moon, and the stars were shining so brightly without any city lights to compete with them. Gazing up at the Southern Cross, I couldn't believe how lucky I was to be experiencing such tranquility, far from civilization and the chaos that often accompanied it.

After returning my car to the city, Rumbidzai and I traveled by bus to stay with her brother and his family in a high-density area known as Chitungwiza. When we arrived at the main bus terminal in the capital city, crowds of people were surging toward the openings of each overflowing vehicle. People were shouting and pushing from all directions. Rumbidzai shoved me in front of her and guided me in the right direction while I tried awkwardly to cling to my overnight bag. In a sea of black, I suddenly felt self-conscious, my own stark white skin blaring in the sun.

At the mission, I had always felt welcome because everyone there was used to visitors coming from other countries. Now, pulling myself up through the doorway of the bus, I realized how far out of my element I had come. I felt the stares, yet I couldn't understand one word being said around me. Shrinking into my seat like a small child, I was glad to have Rumbidzai beside me. A man said something to her in Shona, and it seemed at once as if the whole group hushed, waiting for her answer. A moment later, the tension broke into laughter and smiles. With one small gesture, Rumbidzai had somehow managed to get an entire busload of Zimbabweans to accept me.

"What did he ask?" I questioned her quietly.

"He wanted to know if you were my daughter-in-law," she answered.

"What did you tell him?" I asked, a smile now growing on my face.

She laughed back, "I told him yes, of course, and we were going to see your husband!"

Chitungwiza was one of the places people had warned me was too dangerous, yet I was greeted and welcomed into a loving family. Everyone in the community went out of their way to make us feel at home. Rumbidzai's brother and sister-in-law gave up their only bed and stayed on the floor at a neighbor's house just so we would have a comfortable place to sleep. They bought and cooked food that was over their monthly salary, and it was some of the best food I have ever tasted.

We went to visit with a pastor nearby, and before we prayed at the end, I heard them sing "*Mwari Mubatsiri Wedu*" for the first time. This song, "God Is Our Helper," was one of Rumbidzai's favorites, so she spent extra time teaching me the words. The first day after I arrived back at Fairfield, I was an instant hit when everyone at devotions realized I knew the words to that song. The mothers knew from that point on that I cared about learning their culture, songs, and language, and I was very grateful Rumbidzai had given me such a good introduction.

I was quickly thrown back into life at the mission and the following week attended my first Zimbabwean funeral. A four-year-old child had passed away just after being brought to Fairfield. I had never met him because he had died over three months before

I arrived in Zimbabwe. As often happened, the body had been kept in the mission morgue up the hill from the hospital for many months while the authorities attempted to locate any living relatives and inform them of his death. When none could be found, the responsibility fell on the Fairfield staff to bury the boy at the mission.

We all formed a single line following Dzawanda, our gardener, as he carried the tiny coffin up the hill behind the children's homes. We all sang as we made the ascent to the top, and when we reached the place where the grave was being dug, I noticed other tiny mounds of dirt and rock surrounding me, each signifying a life that had ended too quickly. This, I would later find out, was the special graveyard for infants, and most of them were unmarked. It was impossible for any of us to stop the tears from flowing as two mothers lowered his miniature box into the ground, with the beautiful sounds of Shona hymns enveloping us.

After sharing that experience with the mothers at Fairfield, the place began to feel more like a real home to me. Each morning I woke up and walked onto the front porch to be greeted by the mothers who were already busy hanging laundry on the line. Mai Mari Jeni would call to me from house one, *"Mangwanani, muroora,"* meaning "Good morning, daughter-in-law." This was used as an affectionate term, and it made me feel like I was part of the community.

I had learned from my stay in the rural areas that a daughter-in-law is expected to do a lot of the work, so I tried my best to be a good *muroora* each day, learning to wash my clothes better by hand, hanging them to dry, washing dishes, sweeping, mopping, and polishing the clay floors of our house. It seemed no matter how much I did, there were always dozens of chores that still needed to be done. Cecilia, more experienced at housekeeping, often took up the slack for me. More often than not, I was on dish duty, not yet able to master the art of cooking *sadza* for our meals.

Each afternoon when the children returned from school, I would walk into the courtyard that ran down the middle of the two rows of homes. Some of the older children would already be waiting and would begin yelling that it was time for jogging, which basically meant we sprinted for about twenty seconds and then walked the rest of the way around the mission. But my favorite part came right before we left for our jog.

Out from house three, my little boy Tendai would often peek around the corner of the doorway. His eyes lit up each time he saw me. I would lean down with arms wide open, waiting as he tottered toward me on his still unsteady two-year-old legs. It amazed me that no matter what type of day I was having, a child's laughter seemed to make it all worthwhile— especially laughter from Tendai, who just two years before had been struggling to survive as we raced him to Mutare General Hospital.

During one of our daily jogs around the dirt path on the mission, a little girl wrapped her fingers around my left hand and began walking beside me.

She stopped after a few minutes and looked up at me. I discovered why only after I noticed blood pouring out of her left pinky finger. The tall dry grass rising on either side of the path had sliced a deep gash that made me want to cry out in pain just to look at it.

As I began wrapping a piece of her dress around the wound to stop the heavy bleeding, I was saddened for two reasons. First, she never made a sound or shed one tear, but just kept staring at me with glazed-over eyes. What had this five-year-old experienced in her short life that enabled her to endure this much pain without even flinching? It also saddened me, as I watched my own hands become stained with her blood, that I even had to consider checking myself for open cuts in case the little girl was HIV positive. I knew that in Zimbabwe, there was a very good chance that she was.

Chapter 7

Moving Forward

My presence will go with you,
and I will give you rest.
— Exodus 33:14

Almost immediately I began to notice changes in the children as they adjusted to living in the new homes. Whereas at the orphanage they had been dirty, malnourished, and lacking attention, now they were truly living as a family. They took care of their brothers and sisters and followed their mother's instructions. The children were now bright-eyed, happy, and full of joy. They were doing better in school. They were clean and well fed. The babies could always be found wrapped securely on their mothers' backs instead of lying for hours in their cribs. Although they had already become my family, they no longer needed my direct care.

I struggled during those first few months, trying to discover what my specific purpose would be now that the children at Fairfield were doing so well. It seemed my only options were to stay at Fairfield or look for a place to start a new orphanage. Fortunately, God began providing opportunities that would reveal options I had never considered.

One of my friends was leaving the country and introduced me to a woman named Mai Chimbo. Together they had started an emergency relief project, offering assistance to orphaned children at Guy farm, which was about five minutes from the mission. Each farm in Zimbabwe had an area where the workers and their families lived in huts clustered together on a piece of the farmland to form a small village. As the middle generation began dying from AIDS, the orphans remained behind, living on the farm with older relatives or on their own. These children were often more vulnerable to abuse, neglect, malnutrition, and disease.

Mai Chimbo lived on the mission and worked at the high school there. She had helped care for her sister before she died from the AIDS virus years before. It had affected Mai Chimbo deeply, and she continued to care for her sister's two orphaned children. She was now determined to help others who were suffering from the virus, as a way to keep her sister's memory alive.

Mai Chimbo envisioned expanding beyond Guy farm and the mission to other surrounding farm areas where hundreds of orphans lived. She realized that there was much need for assistance in the form of medical care, nutrition, and education for the families she visited, but the resources available were not enough for the ever-increasing population of orphans and those who were HIV positive. I immediately felt that this was the woman I was to work with. She had a kind heart and in the following years would teach me about patience, kindness, and unconditional love for people whom many others had forgotten.

I traveled with Mai Chimbo to ten farms, where she introduced me to health-care workers who would assist us as we started visiting families every week. The workers had been trained to administer medications for minor illnesses and to report any serious problems in their area to the farm manager. They became invaluable resources to us, able to tell us when people were sick, which children could not afford school fees (there is no free education in Zimbabwe), or if there were malnourished children who needed extra food.

Most of the families we met had at least one member dying of AIDS, tuberculosis, or both. Mai Chimbo explained that if the adults in a family died, the children were left orphaned, with no relative to care for them. Many of the children in the families were already orphaned and were being looked after by a sick aunt or grandmother. Other children were living in child-headed households. Through Mai Chimbo's explanations, I began to realize how important it was to care for the entire family. If we could help the mother or aunt stay healthy, she would live longer to better care for the children.

One of the first days, we went to the home of a young man clearly dying of AIDS. It was the first time I had seen a grown person in the last stages of the disease. His skin barely covered his thin bones, and the skin around his face was pulled so tightly that his teeth were exposed. He could barely speak to us, his thin legs drawn up close to his chest, mouth gaping open from the sores around his lips. I went away shocked and disturbed by what I had seen. With this man's image frozen in my memory and that of the children we had seen suffering in silence, I knew I wanted to work more closely with those who where HIV positive.

After only a few weeks, we started to see an improvement in the families we were working with, as we delivered fruit, eggs, peanut butter, and an immune-boosting porridge. One woman was helping care for a newly orphaned boy a little over the age of two who was so malnourished that he looked smaller than a healthy one-year-old. When I held my arms out to him, he clung to me, and when I handed him a banana, the wailing from his hunger pains was quieted for a little while.

During another visit to pass out donated clothing, we handed a warm sweater to a seventy-six-year-old grandmother. She began dancing and singing all the way back to her hut, where she and her husband cared for their orphaned grandchildren. This old *ambuya* (grandmother) would come to be known affectionately as Dancing Grandmother, dancing and singing each time we visited her. As so many other grandparents, she had lost every son and daughter to the deadly AIDS virus. With no other choice, she was forced back to work, trying to survive with her grandchildren. One family at a time, we were trying to show God's love and make a difference.

Toward the end of July, my car began giving me problems. I went into town with a friend, and we dropped it off to be fixed at the local mechanic's shop. We walked back into the center of town to run some errands and stopped beside a car parked on the main road to talk to some people we knew. Out of the corner of my eye, I saw a young man running toward us, but instead of going past, he headed straight for me. The look on his face scared me. There seemed to be something evil in it that I would not see often during my time in Zimbabwe.

The next thing I knew, he lifted his leg, kicking me into the car. As quickly as he had come, he turned and ran away. Everyone on the street around us stopped and stared, but after a few minutes everything returned to normal. I tried to laugh it off, knowing there were still tensions between the different racial groups in Zimbabwe that ran back many generations. I had just been placed in the middle of it. I wondered how many times in my life I had made snap judgments about people I did not know.

When I returned to pick up my car at the end of the day, my bill was a shocking Zim$200,000 which was only US$40. The rate had now grown to Zim$5,000 to every US$1. The owner of the shop saw the large bruise already starting to form on my upper arm from where the man had kicked me. She asked what had happened, and by the end of our conversation, she had invited me to the church she attended in town. I promised to meet her there the following Sunday.

As I walked through the doors of the church a few days later, people of all different nationalities filled the building. A man named Richard, who was about my age, was being introduced. He had returned to Zimbabwe to visit his parents. After talking briefly with me after the service, he invited me to meet his family later in the week. It turned out that his father was Dave Meikle, the owner of Meikle farm, where Mai Chimbo and I had just begun working to help the orphans. White farmers still ran most of the farms in our area, many of which had been threatened by the government as it continued the land redistribution that had started in 1998. The few farmers who were still working were constantly in a state of unease, not knowing when they would be forced to leave.

I put on my nicest outfit, complete with the bleach marks from my many failed attempts to wash clothes properly in Cecilia's bathtub, and drove my little Mitsubishi to Meikle farm. As I turned down the dust road, mountains rose up on all sides, and I arrived at a small entrance shaded by beautiful flowering trees. I felt so self-conscious pulling into the driveway of the large nineteenth-century farmhouse. It was as if I had stepped into another world, hearing Richard's mother ask me in her delicate accent if I would like some tea. I was handed a china cup like my great-grandmother had passed down to us, with a tiny spoon to stir in the sugar and a biscuit (cookie) placed on the saucer sitting underneath the cup.

After months immersed in the Shona world, where I slurped tea from mugs and used my hands to eat a side order of giant yams, I didn't know quite what to do with myself. Richard and his family were very polite, and over the next two weeks I was invited into a world I had previously been unaware existed in Zimbabwe. I attended *brais* (barbeques) with their relatives and friends, met Richard's frail but clever grannies at the nursing home, and took drives all over Mutare to places I had never seen before. One evening we drove high up a mountain that over-looked Mutare. It was so beautiful watching the tiny lights from the houses below blur into the night sky. It looked like we were watching an entire fleet of sailboats floating out across black, inky water.

Richard explained that his relatives had come down through Africa on wagons in the 1800s, stopping all along the way and setting up stores. Now all over Africa, including Zimbabwe, there were Meikle department stores and hotels. His family owned the farm where they now lived. They had experienced much persecution during their lifetime. Throughout the war that ended in 1980, his family often had to maneuver around land mines planted along the dirt road leading out of their house, just praying that they would not hit one.

Many times in the last years, as farms were being taken by the government, the Meikles had been threatened. They used to own three very large farms when Richard was growing up, and all the mountains that surrounded them had been his backyard playground, complete with a rock fort that overlooked his estate.

Slowly, over the years, the government had forced them to give up pieces of their land until they were now left with only their house and about 20 percent of one farm.

I learned over those two weeks that the farmers in our community were hardworking people who loved their families and their country and showed amazing faith during the difficult times they had faced. Most of them had been there for many generations and had fairly purchased the land where they lived. After Richard left, I continued to see his parents once a week at a Bible study held by Jane and Larry Keis. Larry was a missionary from the States and had lived in Zimbabwe for many years. His wife was originally from Botswana, and together they had four children. We had a lot of fun every Thursday evening with our little group, singing songs and sharing stories. It was nice to escape the difficulties of everyday life and enjoy tea and laughter with these newfound friends.

*   *   *   *   *

Although my Zimbabwean family was growing, life was not going well for my family back home. My grandfather, Buddy, had been diagnosed earlier in the year with cancer. His health was rapidly deteriorating. One night my mom called in a panic, saying that Buddy had only a few days to live. After several failed attempts to schedule a flight out, I called my grandfather. Walking outside as the moonlight shimmered and the cool night air blew around me, I heard my grandfather's voice for the last time.

That night my grandfather slipped peacefully away. All my relatives agreed they would postpone the funeral until I flew home. I now had a big decision to make. Plane tickets to the States were not cheap. I asked one of my Zimbabwean friends what I should do. He reminded me that the word *kumusha* means a person's rural home where parents or grandparents live. Zimbabweans go *kumusha* for family gatherings and celebrations. If it is at all possible, they return *kumusha* when there has been a death in the family so that they can comfort one another.

As I thought about what he had said, I made my decision. I had tried my best over the first months to learn and follow the customs and culture of Zimbabwe. I had come to learn that the Shona people place importance of family second only to God. I realized it was the same with my family. The most African thing I could do was go *kumusha* and be with my family. I thanked God that day, so far away from home, that the things of this earth that could destroy a human body could not touch the soul.

Chapter 8

The Least of These

Wherever there is a human being, there is an opportunity for kindness.

—Lucius Seneca
First-century Roman philosopher

When I returned to Zimbabwe a few weeks later, the project I had been working on with Mai Chimbo seemed to take off. We were given a significant donation from a family in the States and were now able to make a real difference in some of the more desperate cases. Many of the families we assisted were unable to afford school fees or food because their ailing health prohibited them from finding work. Mai Chimbo and I hoped to empower these women and men in the farm areas by assisting them with proper food and medicines so that they would be fit enough to work for their families. We also knew that in the meantime, the children needed more immediate assistance with school fees so they could have some stability each day. As we started to act on the emergency needs we saw, we could see hope returning into the lives of the families we worked with. We decided to call our project HOPE, which stood for "Helping Orphans Providing Empowerment."

Mai Chimbo and I, along with our friend Mai Mashiri, started visiting the farms on a more regular basis. We would leave the mission, pile into my beat-up yellow car, and bump our way down the dusty road. Pulling left onto the main tar road, we would pass a small "tuck shop," where we would stop for a Coke, bread, or snacks before heading out for a long afternoon.

Guy farm was always our first stop, being only five minutes down the road. I would maneuver my car carefully down an embankment on the side of the road, safely out of the way of the other few cars that might venture past. We then walked over rocky paths that eventually narrowed, winding in and out between clusters of huts. Spread out before us was a beautiful scene that never ceased to take my breath away.

Large mountains loomed as a perfect backdrop, covered during different times of the year with bright red, orange, or purple flowering trees. Tiny huts were scattered throughout the valley below. Clusters of men sat on clay stoops outside each wooden door, talking or working on various tasks. Women with worn but colorful wraps covering their clothing moved slowly up the paths, with large containers of water balanced carefully on their heads. Others were bent over, stirring large pots of *sadza* that rested atop black iron grates sitting over the outdoor fires. Children ran and played, shrieking with laughter until they were given a chore to do by one of the adults.

As soon as the children spotted us coming down the hill, one of them would run off to retrieve the health-care worker, who was usually hard at work in the fields. Dressed in blue coveralls with rubber boots that reached to his knees, he always came promptly to greet us, a humble smile covering his face. His job, like the jobs of the other health-care workers on the surrounding farms, was to know the living situations of each family on his farm and to report anything that raised concern. We would sit on a wooden bench outside his hut, and he would brief us on anything new that was happening. From there we would set out to visit each of our families.

Mai Mberi was one of the first women we started visiting at Guy farm, which I later found out had the highest number of HIV-positive patients in the surrounding area. Mai Mberi had gone to the hospital for chest X-rays, and they confirmed she was positive for TB, a common side effect of AIDS. Almost everyone in Zimbabwe was given a vaccine to prevent tuberculosis when they were young, but if AIDS attacked their immune systems, the vaccine was no longer able to offer protection. Therefore, if a person had active TB, we could assume that the person was also HIV positive. Since she had active TB, Mai Mberi had been admitted to the mission hospital to monitor her medicines and was placed on the hospital bill for Project HOPE. She had two daughters and a young grandson who were supposed to be looking after her during her hospital stay.

After a few days, I heard that Mai Mberi had left because the food tasted bad. Not understanding much about the culture or the nature of her disease, I decided that if she was going to be that picky when we were paying her bills, then maybe we needed to move on to another family. After all, her daughter worked to earn money, so I told Mai Chimbo that maybe it was time for Mai Mberi to start looking for work to help herself. Mai Chimbo just looked at me and said calmly, "I think maybe you should come with me to visit Mai Mberi. You haven't seen her in a few weeks."

We went that afternoon, and when I saw her, my heart broke. She lay on a rotting mattress inside her tiny hut and was so frail. We could barely hear her when she tried to talk. It turned out the real reason that she had left the hospital was that her daughter couldn't take care of her there and still keep her job. At the hospitals in Zimbabwe, a patient had to have a relative help prepare food and provide care in order to stay overnight. Since her daughters were not able to do this, they brought her home. We decided to take her back for a checkup the following day.

The next day Mai Chimbo and I entered her hut and together lifted her small frame and hoisted her limp body through the door and onto the back of her thirteen-year-old daughter. The daughter carried her mother like a baby on her back all the way to the car. Mai Mberi came home with a bag full of pills and medications. We tried providing food, but often the children ate the food or prepared it in the morning and left their mother alone all day. Her sickness was too much for them to handle at such a young age.

Nothing made a difference by that point. She was already too sick, her body quickly deteriorating and wasting away. I received word on a Thursday morning that she had passed away the night before. I kept going over and over the situation in my mind. What could we have done differently?

We went to pay our respects to the family, and Mai Mberi's mother said the church members had each provided one board so that together they were able to construct a coffin in which to bury her daughter. She explained they were all relieved that Mai Mberi had come to know Jesus right before she passed away.

I remembered that the last time I saw her, we had prayed in her hut. I had felt a peace as we sang to her, and I sensed God's presence in that room. Maybe I could have done something differently, but God was able to do His work with or without me, and I had learned a valuable lesson: time is precious. I had to learn from the experience and ask God for strength to try again. I would soon find out that He was going to give me many more chances in the near future.

Soon after Mai Mberi's death, I had driven into town and was headed back to the mission. The mission was located in Old Mutare, the site of the original city. Years before, a man named Cecil Rhodes had come through, trying to continue the railroad he was building through this area of Africa. He decided it would be easier to build it on the other side of a

large mountain range known locally as Christmas
Pass, named when early settlers walked over it on
Christmas morning. Cecil moved the entire town of
Mutare to the other side of this mountain, where it
now remains, and eventually gave a large portion of
the old land, Old Mutare, to the United Methodist
Church, where the mission and Africa University
were built.

As I reached the summit of Christmas Pass that
day, I was again awed by the spectacular view of
the city below. The purple jacaranda trees had just
begun to bloom all over the city, and they created
a beautiful and peaceful view on my drive over the
mountain. Turning right once I reached the bottom, I
smiled as my eyes passed over the odd-shaped tops
of the mountain ranges in the distance. I was almost
home.

Mai Chimbo stopped by as I was unloading the
groceries from the car and convinced me that we
needed to visit a man named Baba waBenji (father of
Benji), who lived at the far end of the mission. She
had been skirting the issue for a few weeks, but I had
conveniently ignored the hints she laid down. The
thought of spending my afternoon with a sick adult
man did not sound appealing to me. Mai Chimbo,
however, had a quiet way of patiently revisiting
certain situations until I finally caught up with her
spirit of concern. As usual, when I finally listened
to her, it was my heart that changed and my life that
benefited from the visits that were to follow.

We started out from Mai Chimbo's house,
together with Mai Mashiri, toward the middle of

the afternoon. Walking down the dusty road, we joked and passed around the usual gossip that I had quickly realized was central to mission life. After a few minutes, we came to a narrow dirt trail leading to a cluster of shacks I had never seen before. A steady flow of sewer water blocked our path, but we managed to negotiate our way safely to the other side with the help of a well-placed concrete slab. On our left, water spilled from a tap where a young mother stood bent over on a pile of rocks, washing pots from the afternoon meal. Her children were scattered around her, watching us intently as we passed. A few yards farther on our right, we came to a two-room house with cracks forming from the ground.

Greeting the onlookers on the surrounding stoops, we ducked into the door nearest us. It took a few moments for my eyes to adjust to the darkness, but the unpleasant smell of sickness hit my nostrils immediately. As the room came into view, I saw a small wooden table in the center and two long, narrow benches along the wall. There was a sheet dividing the room in half, and from the other side of where we stood, I heard the rustling of someone getting up from a bed. The curtain parted, and a thin, hunched-over man shuffled toward us, his mouth gaping open, a glazed look in his eyes. He was swallowing hard and working just to breathe.

In a painful procedure, he managed to sit on the edge of one of the benches, gesturing for us to do the same. We could now see clearly, and it was hard to avoid noticing the filth that surrounded us. Crumbs of food were scattered across the table and onto the floor. The walls were covered with black grime, the curtains tinged brown.

After the traditional greetings and polite conversation, we all sat in silence, shuffling our feet against the cement floor. Having left our shoes on the mat at the doorway, I could feel the cold seeping through the balls of my feet and into my legs. Mai Chimbo began speaking to Mai Mashiri fervently in hushed tones. They both looked to me, and I could tell that what was coming next would probably situate me somewhere far outside my comfort zone.

"We were thinking to come back tomorrow to clean the house. Baba waBenji only has his two children to look after him, so maybe some of the neighbors will pitch in and help," Mai Chimbo said.

I took another quick glance around the room, the slightest sense of dread creeping into my stomach. I had to be taught how to push the buttons on a washing machine, just before going off to college. Every time I thought to offer to help my mom rinse dirty dishes before placing them safely in the dishwasher, I thought better of it. I had never vacuumed our house a day in my life, and yet here before me was a task that I felt sure would involve no electrical appliances for assistance. This fact became crystal clear in my mind, as my eyes frantically swept the room for signs of outlets. But there was no electricity and no running water. The answer, however, was clear. Here sat our brother, whose blood relatives had abandoned him. We saw no other hands and feet but our own.

After singing and praying together with Baba waBenji, we asked if we might come back tomorrow and explained our plans. He agreed and forced himself to stand to see us off before pushing through the curtain to seek rest in his bed. As we left the room, I breathed in deeply the fresh outside air.

From around the corner of the house came two sullen children, their dark clothing dirty and torn, reflecting their obvious mood. They stared at us suspiciously. This was the first time I met Benji and Chipo, Baba waBenji's eleven- and eight-year-old children. I knew nothing at that time of the relationship God had in store for us. Chipo had been busy washing blankets in a bucket while Benji gathered vegetables from the garden in order to start cooking dinner. Mai Chimbo later explained that these two children were the sole caregivers for their father. It was Benji who cleaned out the bucket when his father threw up in the middle of the night. It was tiny Chipo who came home from school each day only to find more soiled blankets to rinse. Their childhood had been taken from them the moment their father became ill.

On the way home, I asked Mai Chimbo about the mother. "No one has seen her for a long time, and it has been their father who has always looked after them." Now, I thought to myself, it was the other way around.

The three of us reported for duty late the next afternoon after Mai Chimbo had finished work, complete with buckets, bleach, mops, and brooms. Mai Chimbo had asked every person in the area if they would come and help us, but only one woman came. It was at that moment that I understood how deeply stigma had worked its way into the society. I had heard rumors of people being shunned by friends and neighbors because of their HIV status, but here I was experiencing it firsthand.

Fear can be deadly for everyone concerned. I later found out that no one would even come to visit Baba waBenji, let alone be directly involved. People were afraid to touch his few possessions or be near him, because they feared they might also get sick. They were afraid that if they were seen with him, others would assume they also had the disease.

I was honored and humbled that day to work alongside three women who truly took Jesus' command to love one another to a higher level. We worked silently into the evening hours as Baba waBenji slept in his bed, the sounds of congested coughing echoing throughout the room at regular intervals. Looking back, I see it as a sort of dance, the way we moved throughout the confined space, each one with her designated chore, as darkness fell around us. Humming to myself as I worked, I thought how much Zimbabwe had changed me in such a short span of time. Everything now in this new place could be seen as an act of worship, rather than a menial task. It emerged vivid and real to me, and as the smell in the room changed from putrid to fresh, I sensed my soul making the first meager signs of the same conversion. It was a feeling of joy. I felt free.

*   *   *   *   *

Zvakaoma . . . life is hard. This is an expression used often in Shona culture, meaning something similar to "it is too hard to handle at this time." In the days that followed my introduction into the joys of cleaning, I started to understand this phrase a little better.

Baba's situation worsened until finally he had to be admitted into the mission hospital. I decided I should take a picture of the children with their father so that they would have a copy. Benjamin and Chipo came to my house about five thirty one evening, just as it was beginning to get dark. Our electricity was out again, now a common occurrence, so we trekked up the little hill toward the hospital as dusk surrounded us. A flashlight beamed light on the path in front of us.

As soon as we entered the main entrance, wailing and screaming filled our ears as a small, limp body was rushed past us and out the door. Benjamin and Chipo had to wait outside while a mother mourned the loss of her baby son who had died just moments earlier. We sat on the porch and watched as they carried the body up to the morgue.

Benji looked at me timidly and asked, "Where do people go when they die?" I asked him where he thought they went.

He thought for a moment and answered, "To heaven, up where the sky is really blue and there are white fluffy clouds."

I said we didn't really know what heaven would be like, but we didn't have to worry about it. If we trusted Jesus, we could know that whatever God had planned for us in heaven would be so much better than anything we could try to imagine.

"It is a place where there is no suffering or tears," I continued, half talking to myself by this point. I could tell the children's minds were inside with their father.

After a while, the sounds from the hospital grew softer, and we walked timidly inside. In the growing darkness, we could barely make out Baba's thin frame. He was attached to an IV and staring straight ahead. My friend Nyasha had accompanied us, and we now pushed the children forward as they greeted their father in Shona. Benji stood looking at his father, and his voice cracked as he began to cry. Baba's voice was barely audible as he answered back a greeting to his son.

We took a picture of both the children with their father and asked him if there was anything special we could bring him the next day. He requested an apple and a Fanta drink. I agreed, all the while knowing that Mai Chimbo would not be happy with me for giving him so much sugar after her multiple lectures on proper diet for those who were ill. We prayed for him, and his mouth breathed a silent amen.

As we walked home, in what had become complete darkness, Nyasha could tell I was upset. She said to me, "Don't worry. God has a purpose." That night as we walked along, I could not see the purpose. There were already millions of orphans in Zimbabwe. There were about to be two more. Chipo and Benjamin were going home to an empty house where there was hardly any food. Baba was suffering alone in his hospital bed, and I felt completely help-less. Everything we did seemed trivial, like throwing a tiny pebble down a deep hole.

Then these words passed through my mind: "Now we see but a poor reflection as in a mirror; then we shall see face to face. Now I know in part; then I shall know fully, even as I am fully known. And now these three remain: faith, hope, and love. But the greatest of these is love" (1 Cor. 13:12–13).

I had to remind myself that God knew Baba fully, loved him fully, and was right beside him while he lay helpless in his hospital bed. If I did not know anything else to do, I could show him by example how much God loved him. I could cover his two chil-dren with that same love.

A few days later, Baba waBenji was driven *kumusha* on a mattress in the back of an open truck. He passed away just weeks after I first met him. Benji and Chipo were taken *kumusha* as well, without the chance for us to even say good-bye. Mai Chimbo and I both felt a great pressing on our hearts to do some-thing for these two children beyond what we were able to do for others. Over the course of knowing them, they had become like part of our family. Now there was an obligation to take care of them as we would our own son or daughter.

Because of the great number of orphans in the country, the only children who could generally be accepted into an orphanage were those who had absolutely no living relatives to take care of them. Benjamin and Chipo were a special case because they still had their mother living, although no one could find her. This ruled out the possibility of moving them to Fairfield Children's Homes. If they lived with their other relatives, they would no longer be able to attend a good school.

After talking through various possibilities, the best solution seemed to be to place them in the mission boarding school. Many children in Zimbabwe attended boarding schools, where they were well looked after and received extra help with their school lessons. With this arrangement, Benji and Chipo would be able to go to their rural home on the school holidays to be with their grandmother.

What at first seemed like a good idea presented us with many obstacles. We had to petition to have Benji and Chipo brought back to the mission and accepted to the boarding school. This meant we had to prove we were financially able to pay the high boarding costs along with all the extra school supplies they would need. After some simple math, the truth was laid out: we would need at least eight sponsors willing to send support every month to keep Benji and Chipo in school. But the decision needed to be made quickly so that the children wouldn't fall behind in school. Each day that we delayed meant an extra day they were without lessons.

We decided to act in faith and sign the papers for Benji and Chipo to attend boarding school at the mission beginning the following term. In this way, we would be able to make sure they received proper care and counseling, as well as keep them around familiar people and places during the difficult months ahead.

Not knowing where else to turn, I sent a request to everyone back home, explaining the situation and praying that someone would come forward to help. Many people on the mission were also praying in faith that this small miracle would take place. In the manner that God often works, He laid this task on the hearts of six sponsors almost immediately. Within the next week, one more came forward to sponsor both Benji and Chipo, making a total of eight—exactly what we needed, no more and no less. I remain extremely grateful to those eight who proved to me once again that God was in control of the situation. They had been called one by one and proved faithful.

The following week, while walking back to my house, I saw Benji coming toward me with his friend. It was the first time I had seen him since before his father died. His face lit up with a smile of recognition, and he waited for me to speak first. After asking how he was, I said the words I had been hoping would be possible: "Benji, would you and Chipo like to go to boarding school at Hartzell, here on the mission?"

The expression on his face spoke for itself. It was a resounding yes. Benji flew through his boarding school interviews that week with no problems, and Chipo was scheduled for the day after her brother. She came to tell me that her interviews were at ten o'clock, and when I asked her if there was anything else, she looked nervously down at her feet. She said that her parents were invited to attend the interview sessions because she was so young, and then she looked up at me and asked if I would go with her to stand in as her parent. I beamed with pride. That was an appointment I would not miss.

Chapter 9

The Good Shepherd

My cup overflows.

—Psalm 23:5

Over the next months, I was busy preparing all the supplies Benji and Chipo would need to begin boarding school in January, but there were other situations also occupying my time. We had discovered a two-year-old named Tadiwa, living at Five Streams farm, who needed immediate attention. His aunt, Mai Mwoyo, had brought him to my house along with her own son. She explained that Tadiwa's parents had both passed away, leaving him alone. She was now trying to care for him, along with her own two small children. Mai Mwoyo had heard that we were able to help with medical bills for some of the children in the community.

Tadiwa was weak, but he could sit up on my lap and hold toys in his hands. Mai Chimbo and I did what little we could to help. Tadiwa was sent to the hospital and given medicines. We gave him a little milk formula because he had not been able to eat solid food. I also gave him a few outfits that had been donated by the women's group from my church at home.

The family lived rather far away, but we went a few times to visit and bring more milk. Each time Tadiwa seemed to be worse, but the aunt never gave up caring for him. It had been suggested that she breastfeed her nephew instead of her own son so that Tadiwa could have more milk. She followed this advice, sacrificing for this small, sick child, while her neighbors mocked and ridiculed her. Each time we visited her, there were more stories and more tears as she described others' stares and questions as to why she was keeping a sick child in her home.

"They ask me why I am endangering my own family for a baby who is going to die anyway," she once said. Yet she continued to show Tadiwa unconditional love.

One day we entered the hut, and Tadiwa could no longer sit up, his hands clenched into tiny fists. A few days later, a little girl walked up to me and handed me a small piece of paper before turning to run back to school. I always dreaded receiving these little scraps of paper because it is almost always told me the same bad news. This time was no different.

The paper was from Mai Chimbo and read, "Sister Janine, I am sorry to inform you that Tadiwa passed away last night." We were told that church members had arrived that Thursday night to pray that the Lord would either take him or heal him, because he was suffering so much. Their prayers were answered, as just a few hours later on the same day, he passed away peacefully in the arms of Mai Mwoyo.

That night I woke around two o'clock with a melody running through my head that I couldn't quite identify. It was one of the Shona hymns the mothers sang sometimes for morning devotions, but I knew only the first line. After about half an hour, I gave up trying to fall back asleep, switched on my light, and searched my hymnbook for the song. I finally found the one I wanted, "*Jehova Mufudzi Wangu*," from Psalm 23: "The Lord is my shepherd." I began singing the song quietly, and after a while there seemed to be something driving me to continue in my feeble attempt to memorize the long lists of syllables I could barely understand. When I finally dragged myself out of bed at six, I was exhausted, but the song was now mine.

I arrived to pick up Mai Chimbo and Mai Mashiri at seven o'clock sharp, and miraculously, for African time, they were ready to go a mere forty-five minutes later. These two women continued to amaze me, as I watched them work tirelessly to make sure our resources went to the neediest orphans and caregivers. When we went to pay our respects, Mai Mwoyo and her husband asked if we wanted to see Tadiwa's little grave. They said they had buried him the in green "suit" we had given to him (a little pair of pajamas).

While we were waiting for someone to take us, Mai Mwoyo offered us some homemade bread baked on a fire outside. God seemed to provide a little comic relief in the middle of our tragedy as I watched Mai Mwoyo take the knife she had been using outside to cut up a dead chicken, dip it briefly in cold water, and proceed to cut my helping of the bread. She offered it to me with a big smile. What could I do? I prayed quickly for a stomach of iron and took a big bite.

The five of us later walked silently to the place where Tadiwa had been buried a few days earlier. We stood solemnly side by side and were asked to sprinkle a small amount of dirt at the head of the grave. I was told that in Shona culture this is reserved for family members as a way of saying good-bye, but the uncle said we had helped to take care of Tadiwa, so we were now part of his family. As soon as he said it, I again felt the heavy weight of responsibility. Surely there was more we could have done. Had it been my own child, surely I would have done more. I soon was reminded, however, that God was in control. It was not about anything we did or did not do.

Before we said a final prayer for Tadiwa, one of the women began singing a song in the most beautiful, almost haunting voice. Where had I heard it before? It suddenly hit me. I smiled to myself as I joined in the singing of "*Jehova Mufudzi Wangu.*" It was the song the Lord had wakened me that morning to memorize so I could mourn with the others. I no longer felt so out of place, as for the first time God allowed me to fit into the culture He had placed on my heart to love so deeply. The Lord is our shepherd, and at that moment I knew we did not need to fear or doubt anything in this valley of physical death that was surrounding us.

Days later Mai Chimbo and I visited Guy farm, where we checked on Mai Damboka. We had been helping her with bus fare to get to the hospital for her TB treatment. As we were sitting on the stoop outside her hut, she explained that her sister had passed away recently, leaving a little girl and boy in her care. When we asked to see them, Mai Domboka said the boy was playing with his friends. We questioned her a second time about the girl. At this point, she ducked into her hut and retrieved a very frail-looking child who was so malnourished that she fell limp and unresponsive against her aunt.

The little girl, named Faith, couldn't shake our hand or even form words to greet us. We read her medical card with its long list of tests and medicines she needed. At the top of the page, however, in big red letters the doctor had written, "This child is severely malnourished and needs food." The aunt had been too ill to work long enough to provide food for herself, let alone for Faith or her brother. What shocked us most was her age. I assumed she was four or five at the most, but her medical card stated that she was more than eight years old.

We visited Faith a few more times and decided we would be able to pay for her hospital tests. It would be a while before we could get the results back, however, and until then she needed enough food to keep her stable. The next day her aunt came to collect porridge, cooking oil, and peanut butter from us, as well as a large bag of fruit. We also gave her some vitamins that had been sent in a package from the States a few days earlier. We were worried about the food being misused, already aware that there were other family members who needed it as well. In the end, we decided that it was better for Faith to have some food than to have none at all. After seeing Mai Mberi and Tadiwa deteriorate, my spirits were low. Already I was starting to lose hope that we would be able to accomplish anything of value.

One week later, Mai Chimbo and I returned for a follow-up visit. I arrived at the hut first and looked inside, where we were used to seeing Faith lying limply on her aunt's mattress. The bed was empty. My heart fell. I remember thinking, "God, I can't handle another one right now. Please take me away from here." We sat down on the mound outside the hut and waited as Mai Domboka slowly came out from the house and gave us the traditional greeting.

I inhaled deeply and asked, "Faith *aripi?*" which means, "Where is Faith?"

Both Mai Chimbo and I sat there, holding our breath, waiting for the answer that I thought I already knew. All of a sudden, Mai Domboka realized why we were looking so sullen, and a huge smile flashed across her face. She answered, "Faith *arikutamba*" (Faith is playing). I sat stunned, as at that very moment Faith came around the corner with a little bucket of water on her head, smiling like it was the best day of her life.

During the rest of our visit that afternoon, she laughed and danced with excitement, especially when we gave her a little doll to tie on her back. It was a miracle. It was truly like watching someone rise from the edge of death right in front of us. I barely recognized her. She was still severely underweight, but her whole demeanor had changed. The facts did not match up with my reality. It had taken one short trip to the grocery store and about ten U.S. dollars to buy what we had given her. There had to be something else present to have made this kind of transformation. I smiled inwardly, as I thought about my words to God just a few moments before. God was restoring His daughter Faith to health and renewing His other daughter's faith at the same time.

After our visit with Faith, we crossed the tar road to see how a second friend was feeling. I had formed a friendship with this woman, Mai Muchena. She was taking care of her four nieces and nephews after the death of her sister, and I always enjoyed our time together.

The first time I met her she was very ill and sitting on the floor of her hut. Mai Chimbo, Mai Mashiri, and I had ducked inside to find her legs and arms covered in sores. After talking to Mai Muchena for a while, we asked if we could pray with her. By the middle of the prayer, I started to hear weeping. Mai Chimbo prayed mightily that day for Mai Muchena to feel God's presence in her hut and for God to take away all fear she had, restoring her to health. When she was finished, Mai Chimbo asked Mai Muchena why she was crying.

"I had forgotten," she said.

A few months later, I would be at home in the States, sitting across from my pastor. After listening to my heartache over the situations I had experienced over the first six months in Zimbabwe, he would hand

me a paper with words from John Wesley, from the
Book of Offices of the British Methodist Church:

> I am no longer my own, but thine.
> Put me to what thou wilt, rank me with whom
> thou wilt.
> Put me to doing, put me to suffering.
> Let me be employed for thee or laid aside for
> thee,
> Exalted for thee or brought low for thee.
> Let me be full, let me be empty.
> Let me have all things, let me have nothing.
> I freely and heartily yield all things to thy plea-
> sure and disposal.
> And now, O glorious and blessed God, Father,
> Son, and Holy Spirit,
> Thou art mine, and I am thine.
> So be it.
> And the covenant which I have made on earth,
> Let it be ratified in heaven.
> Amen.

As I read the prayer, my hurt began to melt away.
I began weeping and he asked me why I was crying.

"I had forgotten," I answered, my mind flashing
back to this very moment where I was sitting in a
small hut with this great woman of faith. Sometimes
we know the answer to our pain and sorrow. All we
need is a little reminder.

A special bond formed between Mai Muchena
and me during the next few months. Her health stabilized, and soon it was almost time for me to return to

America for a visit. I made Mai Muchena promise me that she would be there when I came back.

A few days later, Mai Chimbo and Mai Mashiri threw a party for me. All their children made up songs and skits about the adventures we had experienced together in the farm areas. It was a true blessing to have made such good friends over the last months.

That Friday, before leaving Zimbabwe, I read the last letter from the stack my friend Julie had given me back in the States. When I left six months earlier, she had handed me a small paper bag with thirty cards inside, one for each week I was going to be away, to give me encouragement. Closing the card with a smile, I quietly placed it back inside the envelope. I had made it through this leg of the journey.

Chapter 10

Lessons in Trust

Sometimes you feel lost, but God knows
where you are.

—Anonymous

That Christmas I quickly reentered the swing of life back home. I traveled in January to a conference held by CornerStone, my mission board. All the missionaries had come home from around the world for a time of sharing, laughter, food, and fun. I was introduced that week to a girl named Melissa, and we became friends right away. She asked all about Zimbabwe, and I casually commented, "You should come sometime." I expected a reflex reaction of dismay, but Melissa didn't falter. In fact, soon after she asked if she could come to Zimbabwe with me for a few months, and we began making plans to return.

Throughout this time, I continued to receive discouraging reports from Mai Chimbo about people who were dying on the farms. Although it was much more difficult this time to say good-bye to my family because I didn't know when I would see them again, the news of these deaths was a driving force drawing me back to the airport. As I headed for the departure gate, I once again felt loneliness take over, and I boarded the plane in tears. It was a relief to arrive in Chicago after my first short flight and see Melissa already waiting there. We enjoyed our last McDonald's hamburgers and prepared for the two long flights ahead.

Standing with Melissa in the line to receive our visitors' visas once we arrived in Zimbabwe, I looked up to the glassed-in balcony of Harare International Airport. This was the place people always waited for their first glimpse of the incoming passengers. The second floor was crowded with people of all ages and nationalities, waiting for the arrival of family and friends. I searched for our friend Lynn who had promised to be at the airport when we arrived and found her waving frantically from the corner of the balcony.

Lynn lived in Maryland and took a two-week trip to Zimbabwe twice a year. This time she had come to visit the children's homes and attend the Africa University graduation ceremonies the two weeks prior and was flying out the same day we were arriving. We were hoping to have enough time to meet for coffee before she flew out, but the moment we made it through customs and out the main doors, she was waiting with a mixed expression on her face. I could tell she was happy to see us, but something else left me with a sinking feeling in my stomach that settled there and would not lift for days.

"Gil has been put in jail," she said immediately, referring to our friend who was a professor at Africa University. During the years he had lived in Zimbabwe as a professor, Gil had assisted a group of orphaned school children in the high-density area of Sakubva, right outside of Mutare. Lynn said that the government had begun to burn down shacks in Sakubva, where Gil's school children lived, leaving many of them homeless. Gil had gone to the site to take pictures of what was happening. While he was there, police confiscated his camera and placed him under arrest. Unfortunately for Gil, his visa had expired, giving them opportunity to hold him in jail. After a few minutes of these hurried explanations, Lynn was whisked through the line and onto her plane.

I had heard a little about the burnings on the news before I left the States. The government had begun a large-scale campaign officially called Operation Restore Order, but it had also come to be known as Operation *Murambatsvina*, or Operation Drive Out Rubbish. Its purpose was to eradicate illegal housing and activities in slum areas, as well as to reduce the spread of disease. This was accomplished by forcibly burning down huts and shacks across the country. The operation had already started in Harare before we arrived, leaving millions homeless. Sakubva was the first of the burnings scheduled to occur in and around Mutare.

Melissa and I tried to be positive about the situation, and toward the end of our drive to the mission, I was again growing excited to see the children at Fairfield. Eventually we began passing the huts at Guy farm. Just before the turnoff, I showed Melissa where my friend Mai Muchena stayed. There were many people gathered outside the hut, leaving me to wonder what was taking place. I found out later that day, after reuniting with Mai Chimbo, that Mai Muchena had kept the promise she made to me before I left, but just barely. I had asked her to be there when I got back, and she had passed away just after my plane landed on Zimbabwean soil. The woman who had been filled with such a spirit of joy and worked so hard to care for her four orphaned nieces and nephews was now gone.

"Welcome back," I thought drearily.

It took me quite a few days to get back into the routine of being in Zimbabwe. Melissa and I moved into the guesthouse at the children's homes, which was next door to Cecilia. After living in Cecilia's lively house filled with good food, soft furniture, and warm company, our house felt empty and lonely and cold. Melissa did her best to cheer me up, reversing the roles, since this was her first time to ever be in Zimbabwe. I was the one who was supposed to be making her feel at home, but I just couldn't.

I could hardly fight back the tears and had a hard time sleeping at night. I kept praying that God would take the heaviness away. I started praying each night,

"Lord, if it is Your will for me to stay, make it impossible for me to go. If it is Your will for me to go, make it impossible for me to stay." I was reminded of the verse, "The Lord will fight for you. You need only to be still" (Ex. 14:14). With that knowledge, I could finally sleep soundly.

We all walked around on eggshells that first week, not knowing what was going to happen. People from the U.S. embassy arrived in government cars, assuring us that Gil would be able to return to the States safely and that they would not leave Mutare until he was released. In the meantime, I found out that my little yellow car would barely start. Melissa got a crash course on Zimbabwean life, helping to push my car down the road as I tried to jump start it each morning. Two or three of the mothers from the homes would hear me trying to start it up and run out to help, dressed in their uniform skirts and aprons. I am sure we were quite a sight for everyone walking by on their way to work.

Not only did Melissa have to deal with my car, but she also had to learn how to wash her clothes in the bathtub and put up with my lack of cooking skills. Also, for the first two weeks, we had no hot water coming from the bathtub faucet. We had to master the art of "bucket bathing" with water heated on the stove. Melissa and I were both elated to discover that we only needed to flip a switch marked "hot water" on the electrical panel in order for the water to heat up before flowing into the bathtub.

I will always be grateful for Melissa's flexibility and humor during those first days. Fortunately, we were rewarded by being invited to participate in a prayer group the second evening by a few of the mothers from Fairfield. It was wonderful to again hear them sing and to see Melissa experience the beautiful harmony of my African mothers.

One evening, after riding home from town on the commuter bus, Melissa and I returned to find a very nice car parked outside Cecilia's house. Cars were rare at the children's homes, so we went over to find out who had come to visit. Inside sat Gil, his belt buckle pulled tightly around his waist to keep his oversized pants from falling. It had been ten days since he had first gone to prison, and he had lost a lot of weight. He looked tired and like he had aged many years since I last saw him. We all sat around him, entranced as he described what it had been like inside the Zimbabwean prison.

He told us that at night they made everyone remove their clothing and sleep on thin mats infested with bugs. What was amazing was the description that Gil gave of the other inmates. They asked him to tell stories from the Bible. They sang songs to encourage one another, and they stuck up for Gil when the police tried to give him a hard time. He said he tried to think of Paul being captured in prison to give him strength. The degree by which his faith had grown during his time in prison was evident.

Gil was given two days to clear out all the belongings he had collected over the past five years and leave the country. To me he sold a priceless gift. Sitting outside the house was the beautiful new silver car we had admired on our way in. "New," of course, meant only ten years old, considering my other car was celebrating its twenty-second birthday. This car was especially rare for Zimbabwe because it was an automatic and even had a CD player and air-conditioning.

The first time I sat behind the steering wheel, I was overwhelmed. It was a miracle, considering that my yellow car had finally stopped for good the day before and refused to start again. Every time Melissa and I got into the car and it actually started, we offered up a big thanks for God's provision. We would now be able to make our regular visits to the farms, as well as go to town to get supplies we needed without fear of breaking down on the side of the road. Although we were very sad to see Gil go, he left us with this huge blessing.

One of the first things we did in the new car was to drive back to the capital city to process my work-visa papers. I was very nervous about taking the papers to immigration. I had heard horror stories about how difficult it was to be approved for a work permit in Zimbabwe. Most people paid a large sum of money to one of the workers in the immigration office to have their visas processed illegally. I had decided that if God wanted me to stay, I would process my papers legally and wait for the outcome.

When we walked in the first time, I went directly to the counter, where a young woman looked through my papers with a furrowed brow. Suddenly her face lit up. She said, "You want to work at Fairfield Children's Homes? I just graduated from Africa University and used to play with the kids there."

She stamped my papers and said to check back in six weeks to see if I was approved. Until then, she said I was free to work in whatever ways I was needed there. When I went to pay my fee for the visa, they only charged me a small portion of what I had been expecting. Melissa and I couldn't believe that the first steps had been so easy. We didn't know at the time that it would be many more months before I would find out the final decision on my work-visa request.

During the first weeks back at the mission, Melissa and I tried our hand at helping in the crèche, or preschool, at the orphanage. The teacher went on leave after a few days, but we were determined to keep the preschool going strong. Our hopes were almost instantly dashed. After only two hours alone with them, most of the thirty children had managed to run out into the road, nearly killing one another, while we haphazardly chased after them.

While we tried in vain to yell reprimands, using the handful of Shona words we knew, most of the mothers came out onto their porches to watch the tragedy unfolding. After a few minutes of laughing at us hysterically, one mother shouted two words, and all the children instantly returned from their death attempts in the road to their respective homes, where they sat like perfect angels. Melissa and I, deciding we had had enough of crèche for the year, walked through our house and into our separate rooms, closing our respective doors and staying inside until the humiliation wore off.

A few weeks later, my new car had become nothing more than an oversized lawn ornament. It doesn't matter how nice your car is, if there is no fuel in the country; it is still not going to run. The government was having a hard time finding enough foreign currency to purchase fuel for the country. In response, Melissa and I became very proficient in using the public transportation system.

The small commuter buses, known as "combis," went back and forth between the mission and Mutare every day, and we would sometimes spend over an hour waiting for one to show up. Returning home in the evenings was especially difficult since everyone needed a ride home after finishing work. In addition, the long absence of fuel soon forced public transportation to a breaking point, as the demand for its services greatly outweighed the supply of buses and cars available.

One evening we waited, along with dozens of others, until we finally managed to flag down the Africa University bus on its way back toward the mission. I sat looking out the window at literally hundreds of cars stretching in lines from each gas station. Many had come days earlier in a vain attempt to find fuel. Fuel shortages affected many different areas in Zimbabwe, including the ability to find basic commodities such as milk, sugar, cooking oil, and bread. Trucks did not have enough fuel to transport the supplies. We could see the effects of this as more and more people were coming forward from the farms with no food to eat or soap to wash their clothes.

After returning home from our bus trip, Melissa and I gathered the few groceries we had managed to collect in town and walked the all-too-familiar path to the mission hospital. We walked through the doors with confidence now, knowing exactly where each of our patients resided.

Baba Dozva lay resting on his small cot, with his wife faithfully at his side. He had admitted to us that he had recently tested HIV positive, his openness highly unusual. They were now the sole caregivers for three orphans as well as their own children. As we talked for a few minutes, he told us that hospital prices were going to nearly double by Friday, inflation continuing to soar. With a glazed look as he stared at his tattered blankets, he thought out loud, giving one voice to the thoughts of many on that day: "My God," he said, "we're all going to die, aren't we?"

I thought of the words from Psalm 10:17–18: "Lord, you know the hopes of the helpless. Surely you will hear their cries and comfort them. You will bring justice to the orphans and the oppressed, so mere people can no longer terrify them" (NLT). This was our promise, as Melissa and I sought to make sense of all that was happening around us. We would keep on praying and waiting to see Him at work.

After a few weeks, some fuel did begin to trickle back into the country. Now that we were back on the road, however, we didn't seem to run into much traffic. The fuel that did come into the country was very expensive. The few vehicles we did see were trucks filled with mattresses, a few pieces of furniture, and some household goods packed in tightly.

It seemed strange at first, until I remembered that many people were being forced to return to their rural areas because their houses had been burned to the ground as Operation Drive Out Rubbish moved closer to Old Mutare. The estimated number of those left homeless by the operation now reached one and a half million out of a total population of eleven million. When it rained, like it did on this day, there was no shelter for them. People just sat on their beds outside, watching as the water soaked through their belongings.

As I was watching the furniture-filled trucks pass by us that day, my mind flashed back to what had taken place in the farms over the last few weeks. We had been continuing our visits to the farms with Mai Chimbo each week and met a mother, Mai Zulu, who had acquired stomach ulcers because she was so concerned for her children's future. Her hut, where she lived with her two children, was to be burned down in Operation Drive Out Rubbish. We were shocked to find out that each of the farms had a specific date when the huts of those who did not work on the farms were to be burned.

Mai Zulu showed us pictures of where they used to live before her husband died. He had a good job, and they celebrated with birthday parties, family gatherings, nice food, and clothing. Now the woman resembled a mere shadow of who she had been in the pictures. When her husband passed away, she was forced to build a hut at Guy farm, working only as a seasonal worker. She now feared that even the little she had would be taken away when the campaign came to Guy farm. We hoped it would never come to that.

Shortly after, Melissa and I were supposed to pick up a young boy and one of the health-care workers, Mai Maposa, from Peplow farm. The boy desperately needed an operation, and we were supposed to help them get through all the paperwork at the hospital. That morning I woke up very sick. Melissa reassured me that she was able to drive confidently on the left side of the road and remembered the way to Mai Maposa's hut.

I fell back asleep for the rest of the day, only waking to hear the door slam shut. I groggily wandered into the kitchen and poured myself a glass of water. Turning back, I saw Melissa standing in the doorway, tears streaming down her face and a look of anger I had never seen from her before. She turned toward me and screamed between sobs, "They burned down every house!"

After calming down, she explained how she had picked up Mai Maposa and the boy and success-fully maneuvered them through the hospital queues (lines) that day. They headed back toward Peplow, first passing through Guy farm where most of our clients lived. As they drove, Melissa began to see soldiers on the left side of the road and large flames rising over the tall grass. One soldier was standing in the middle of the road, checking off names on a clipboard as each home was burned. Plot after plot of land she passed had only the remnants of a hut, with the families, not knowing what to do next, sitting or standing beside each mound of ashes.

Just as Melissa suspected, Mai Zulu and her two children were among those who lost their homes. Dancing Grandmother was also left homeless, along with her orphaned grandchildren. Melissa managed to drop off Mai Maposa and the boy and had to return past the area in order to get back to our house. I could not imagine the fear she must have felt. She said she just drove looking straight ahead until she reached home. That was July 13, 2005—the day our friends lost their homes and possessions.

Only a short time after Melissa came home and told me about the burnings, I received a letter from one of the children in our HOPE program:

Dear Janine,

I was happy to write this letter to tell you about Operation. On Tuesday the policeman come to our area and started burning the people's house. My father said come here to plan, because my family, we're sleeping outsides, but it has been windy and cold.

Yours faithfully,
Winfer Maone (nine years old)

The Maone family, with five children in total, had been among the first to receive support from Project HOPE the year before to help them start generating income on their own. The father had become very ill and no longer able to work, so the mother took over trying to earn money for the family. We had been so proud when we visited them only one week before the burnings and saw that with their extra earnings they had been able to build a third hut for the children to sleep in. They had also been able to pay the children's school fees on their own. But now the only thing left was a heap of ashes, which was where they had slept the previous two nights.

Right after the burnings at Guy farm, a local group came with donated blankets for the victims of the burnings. I traveled around with them for the day and handed out the blankets to each family. It was eerie to walk toward a spot where I used to sit and visit and now see only burned ashes. The families were sleeping right on the ground, even though there were some remains of walls they could have slept behind. They had been given specific instructions not to sleep inside the ruins or rebuild. The homes were burned in July, the coldest month in Zimbabwe. Many of our clients, who had improved in health over the previous months, instantly returned to poor health because of the weather.

Chapter 11

Stepping Stones

*In this life we cannot do great things. We
can only do small things with great love.*
— Mother Teresa

By the time Melissa returned to the States in
August, many of our families from Guy Farm
whose homes had been burned were now resettled in
town, in Mozambique, or with relatives. Although we
could still see the effects, life had definitely settled
down a lot. A team traveled from South Carolina
and brought many items for Project HOPE and Fairfield Children's Homes. Within a few days of their
arrival, boxes started appearing at the post office as
well, with medical gloves, medicines, vitamins, and
stuffed animals sent from home.

I sat one evening in the room where we stored
the supplies, just amazed at God's faithfulness. He
worked through many people to provide to the point

of overflowing for our needs that month, and it really offered a spark of encouragement after we had seen so much devastation the months before. The children who were part of the HOPE program were happy and healthy because of their sponsors' faithfulness to provide for them. It was amazing to remember where they had come from—malnourished, unresponsive, and weak—and to see how God had filled all of them with life and laughter. All of them, that is, except my friend Michael from next door.

Michael and his brother Matthew had come to the children's homes after they were found wandering the streets of the capital city of Harare. Although they had a grandmother living nearby, she had a hard time looking after the boys. At twelve and nine years old, the brothers fended for themselves on the streets. Fortunately, they had been brought to Fairfield through an AIDS clinic that had tried to assist them. Both brothers arrived at the children's homes with letters stating their HIV-positive status. At first I had no idea they were positive. Both seemed to be healthy, happy boys who were adjusting well to having a mother and being part of a family. As I began to watch them more closely, however, it became apparent that they were carrying the disease.

One day I walked by Michael as he was sitting on the veranda of his house. He had a rash covering his head and cracks along the backs of his ears that had pus coming out of them. His nose was bleeding, and he had an enormous lymph node sticking out on the back of his neck. These were classic secondary symptoms signifying that the disease had progressed in its attack on his immune system.

As I looked at him, I remembered how only the week before he had been holding my hand as we walked around the botanical gardens on a field trip with the children. Seeing him in so much pain now, I didn't even take the time to sit down beside him. He had suffered long enough. I knew nothing about the process at the time, except that there were medicines available to those who were willing to be open about their HIV status. I asked Michael if he wanted to get better. He looked miserably up and stated a simple yes.

I went directly to the administrator at Fairfield, Baba Mufute, to ask if he would allow me to take Michael to the hospital in town to see what could be done. "You can try anything you want for him," he said. "I don't think Michael will live more than a few more years anyway, so it can't hurt."

Baba Mufute had seen that Michael was suffering, but like many, he didn't think there was anything else we could do for him beyond providing a comfortable place to live. I was very grateful that day for his willingness to allow me to look for other options. If he had turned me away, many others that followed Michael may not have received the treatment they needed.

I marched straight back to where Michael still sat and ordered him to put on his shoes because we were going to see the doctor. Slightly stunned, he did as he was told, and a few minutes later we were walking toward the mission hospital to ask the doctor for a referral letter to allow us admittance to Mutare General Hospital in town.

The doctor asked me if Michael understood his disease. I told him that up to this point no one had told Michael what was wrong with him, but now the symptoms had become too much to ignore. The doctor patiently explained to Michael how his disease worked. I hung onto every word he said, learning the information for the first time myself, presented in a way that a child could understand.

Basically, Michael had something in his body that was killing all his "soldiers." This is the word the doctor used to describe the number of white blood cells in the immune system that fight off all illnesses from the common cold to more serious infections. People with AIDS don't die from the virus itself, but rather, the virus kills so many soldiers that the body can die from any other illness, like chicken pox, that normally the soldiers would fight off. A lot of Michael's soldiers had been killed by the HIV virus, so his body didn't have many left to fight sicknesses.

Once Michael started taking ARVs, or antiretroviral drugs, the medicine would trap the HIV virus in little boxes so it couldn't hurt any more of his soldiers. His body would then have a chance to make more soldiers to fight off any sickness that came along. While the virus was trapped in the boxes, however, it was still getting stronger. If Michael failed to take his medicine at the correct times, the virus would escape from its box and start killing soldiers at an even faster rate. After the doctor was sure Michael understood what was happening, he handed me the paper giving us permission to go to the hospital in town.

After driving to the Mutare General Hospital later that afternoon, we learned how to maneuver through their complicated and confusing process. Upon entering the main doors, we first had to sit in a very long line just to see the receptionist who stamped the hospital card that allowed us to proceed to our designated doctor. We then found ourselves in yet another seemingly unending line.

Having maneuvered our way through all the lines, we were met with another obstacle. Michael could not go further in the registration process unless he produced papers stating his positive status. Since each of the children came to Fairfield with only a note from social welfare stating that they were positive or negative, I had to find a way to get Michael legal documentation of his disease.

After I made a quick phone call to Baba Mufute to make sure he approved, Michael and I began wandering the streets of Mutare, asking anyone willing to engage in conversation where the nearest testing center was located. As it turned out, we had to walk quite a distance, but finally we came to a small house located behind a metal gate. Inside we waited again until a kind woman finally called us to take Michael's blood. Looking back, I know what a blessing it truly was to be served that same day. I later took children who were turned back because as minors they had to have an accompanying note from their doctors and the consent of their legal guardians before having their blood taken. I guess the testing facilities were learning right along with us back then.

We returned to the hospital, where we handed over Michael's results and were booked for a registration date the next week. We would discover in the weeks that followed what a lengthy process we had embarked upon, as we went for blood tests, X-rays, and urine samples, only to come back again to be told the results and scheduled for another date. We would leave for the hospital as early as six in the morning to battle the outpatient line. We knew if we had our card stamped before the hospital staff began devotions at seven thirty, it was a good day. This meant that when they finished with prayers and announcements, we could race to the front of the opportunistic-infections (OI) line. The nurses, who at first had been guarded, soon saw that we were serious in our aspirations to get Michael through the registration process to the promised land of ARVs.

Eventually Michael was scheduled for his first group-counseling session. A person was required to go to two sessions before commencing on the drugs to make sure they understood the importance of taking their medications at the right times. One missed pill could compromise the immune system and send a person's health spiraling downward. Michael would also need to continue additional counseling as he began taking the drugs.

He still did not really understand what it meant to be HIV positive, and I could tell it was worrying him. The stigma was huge, and schools, in an effort to promote abstinence, used AIDS as one of the consequences. Therefore, the children thought that if a person had AIDS they were "bad," when in reality most children contracted the disease at birth or through abuse.

Upon entering his first counseling session at Mutare General, I knew we were going to have to look for an alternative solution. Michael sat on a little bench sandwiched between adult women whose disease had progressed much further than his own. Many of them asked questions that did not need to be discussed in front of a small boy. He looked so helpless and confused, and as I thought about how much school he was missing in order to travel to town, I resolved to find another solution. Luckily, God provided an answer to prayer quickly in the form of the Volunteer Counseling and Testing Center (VCT). I had not been aware that a center for HIV/AIDS had recently opened on the mission.

Michael's housemother from Fairfield walked up the road with me to find out about it, and we were pleasantly surprised to find an HIV/AIDS counselor available at the clinic, just a few minutes from the children's homes. The facility had taken over the old orphanage building that housed the Fairfield children before the new homes were built. God had taken a place of malnourishment, neglect, filth, and stench and replaced it with something new that was now offering hope to the community, including the children who used to live there.

The coordinator was very kind and patient with Michael, explaining his disease and answering any questions he had. Because the clinic was just beginning, there was no one waiting in line. Michael could simply walk there every day after school and have someone to talk to about his troubles. Every time he came back from seeing the counselor, I could tell a weight had been lifted off his shoulders. I thanked God for providing light at the end of this long and dark tunnel we had walked down together for the past month.

Shortly after, Michael was transferred to the children's unit, the final destination to begin ARV treatment. We walked into the pediatrician's office to find the same doctor who had saved Tendai's life when he was so sick three years before, and I knew we were now in good hands. After a few short weeks of medication, Michael's "soldiers" came back fighting, and his health quickly improved. The lump, rashes, and all other symptoms seemed to disappear overnight, and Michael was ushered safely back to school, leaving me to see where God would show up next.

Feeling very happy with life after Michael's success, I was able to be with Nyarai as she celebrated her twelfth birthday. It was hard to believe that I had known her since she was just five years old. We were dancing, singing, eating, and laughing inside house ten at Fairfield when an urgent knock was heard at the door. Linda, Fairfield's secretary, had a sister staying at her house who was vomiting and in a lot of pain. She was overdue to give birth, and I had been walking with her up and down the mission road every day on doctor's orders to try to entice the baby to come into the world. We drove her sister up the dirt road to the hospital, and after she received a quick check from the nurse, we found out it was time for the baby to join us. What appalled me was that Linda said good-bye to her sister and started walking out the door.

"You're just going to leave her here by herself?" I asked in disbelief. I could hear her crying out in pain from the other room.

"Yes," Linda said, "the nurses will take good care of her."

I had just discovered another cultural difference, remembering hospitals at home filled with nervous relatives awaiting the birth. I reluctantly followed her home, but by five the next morning, I woke to my alarm clock bright and early in order to go see if the baby had arrived. Mai Chimuka, the mother from house ten, accompanied me as we quietly entered the maternity ward. I knocked lightly at the nurses' station, and a woman asked from behind the door, *"Ndiani?"* (Who is it?)

I answered, *"Janine na Mai Chimuka wekuFairfield."*

"Oh," she said, "you've come to see your baby."

We walked down the hallway and into a room that held three new mothers. Linda's sister was bathing in the other room, but her tiny baby girl was wrapped tightly and lay on the bed. I picked her up and looked up to see her mother walking slowly and painfully toward us.

"What is her name?" I asked.

"Janine Tatendwa," she answered, her middle name meaning, "we give thanks."

I could see a slow smile spreading across her face. I knew I would love this baby forever.

By half past five, I had to leave baby Janine with her mother, who was now known as Mai Janine, or mother of Janine. I had been invited to attend a weekend church conference with one of the pastors on the mission. With six of us in total, the women rode in the back of an open truck for the entire five hours south to the meeting place near Masvingo. That day was filled with preaching, singing, and conversations around me almost entirely in Shona. I slept on a cold cement floor that night with about twenty other women all around me.

When it seemed like I had just found sleep, I heard rustling and women beginning to sing in low voices, *"Mangwanani, Baba"* (Good morning, Father). This was a far more comforting way to wake up than what I remembered from my church sleepovers as a youth member when "This Is the Day the Lord Has Made" was barely audible behind the pan my youth leader was banging over my head. More singers now joined in, and I figured they were getting ready to go back to the second day of the conference. I had already made plans to sleep in and join them later, since I had no idea what was being said anyway.

The singing continued for a long time until I finally cracked open one of my eyes to see what was going on. To my surprise, all twenty women were fully dressed, sitting on top of their neatly tidied blankets, staring at me. I begrudgingly pulled myself to a sitting position, silently vowing to never attend an overnight function anywhere again as long as I lived. As soon as I was upright, the singing immediately stopped, and a woman began to pray. Shortly after, they all filed out into the darkness to begin the day. I looked at my watch that read 4:12 a.m. They had been waiting for their American sister so that we could all join in morning prayers together before beginning the day.

Safely back home the next day, it was time to prepare for yet another journey. Baby Janine was going *kumusha* so that her mother could learn from the *ambuya* how to care for her first child. I was privileged to carry the small baby up the steep, rocky mountainside to reach their huts at the top.

It was going to be a busy day for Linda and me, since we were the only unmarried girls there. It was our job to do all the cleaning, cooking over a fire, carrying water from the well, and any other chores that needed to be done. These duties would fall more heavily on Linda, since I still had little clue as to what I was doing when I visited the rural areas. I watched Mai Janine walking with a stick so she wouldn't fall over from the pain she was still experiencing. Seeing both women made me realize how strong Zimbabwean women had to be in so many different ways.

The next morning around four, I was awakened by baby Janine's cries of hunger, but I happily remembered that her mother was right beside her to feed her. How fortunate to have a mother's comfort in a place where so many did not! With this knowledge, I drifted happily back to sleep.

My early mornings continued, as I arose at a quarter to four that Monday morning to prepare to leave for Harare. My visa had still not been approved, and I had to make yet another trip to immigration. Luckily, a kind officer there gave me a sixty-day extension while I awaited their response. I knew I would sleep well that night, knowing that God had allowed me to stay safely into October in this place I had come to love so much. I hoped this would be my last week of early mornings for a long time.

*   *   *   *   *

One afternoon about a week later, I was standing in the middle of the playground at the children's home, pushing Tendai on a tire swing. A warm breeze passed by as I looked out over the landscape and caught a glimpse of Africa University nestled among the mountains that surrounded us. A child came running up to me, a small slip of paper in her hand, and I again experienced the sinking feeling of déjà vu. The letter was from Mai Chimbo, saying that Mai Domboka, Faith's aunt, had passed away the evening before.

We went to her hut, where all the relatives and friends had begun to gather. Ducking inside, we waited for our eyes to adjust before kneeling in front of her mother and paying our *chema*. *Chema* in Shona means "cry," but it is also used to describe the money given to the closest relative to share in their sorrow and help pay for the funeral costs. A while later we walked behind the tractor that pulled a flatbed carrying her coffin and a large group of people to the place where she would be buried.

Afterwards, people filed past Mai Chimbo and me to thank us for the help we had given Mai Domboka. I couldn't help wondering if we were actually doing any good. The numbers were steadily increasing: Baba waBenji, Mai Mberi, Tadiwa, Mai Muchena, and now Mai Domboka. They had died on my watch, but as I looked out over the dozens of people who had gathered to pay their respects, I had to thank God that they had been well loved.

Chapter 12

Prayers Answered

One single grateful thought raised to heaven
is the most perfect prayer.

—G. E. Lessing
From Laura Moncur's
"Motivational Quotations"

Fortunately, just when the weight of responsibility started to feel too heavy, God showed up and provided for refreshment and renewal. I was invited to go with the Meikles and the Keises to Mozambique for a week. After a long two-day drive on broken tar roads as we sat on a mattress in the back of a pickup truck and eased over potholes the size of craters, we arrived at Pomene, a long stretch of beach on the Indian Ocean. I slept in a little tent right beside the water and fell asleep each night listening to the ocean waves beating against the shoreline.

My friends taught me to appreciate nature a lot more, as we explored tiny aquariums formed among the craters where the tide went in and out every day. The children found puffer fish and figured out how to make them puff up and then sent them floating across the top of the water. We saw flocks of flamingos in the hundreds, and every once in a while, a whale's tail popped out of the ocean—although it was usually when I was busy blinking! On one end of the beach, we explored ruins of an old hotel that had been destroyed by the war in Mozambique years earlier. At high tide as we stood on the edge of the cliff beside the buildings, the huge swell of waves would crash over us, almost knocking us over.

We met Rod and Ellie Hein there on the beach. They had been missionaries from Zimbabwe to Mozambique for many years. A year before, I had been given a book they had written, so I felt like I was meeting celebrities. They had just come with their team and had already been given land by the chief to build right beside the beach. Within months we would receive word that they had built a small chapel, among other buildings, and were making a huge impact on the people native to the area.

I returned to Zimbabwe, ready to begin my work again with renewed energy. There were many children and mothers to hug. It was such fun to laugh with Mai Chimuka and the other mothers at Fairfield. They had all become such good friends. In just a week's time, it seemed my children had grown up, and I now started to notice how much Nyarai was beginning to look like a young woman, beautiful and strong.

My friend sent a text message from the United States that day saying a huge hurricane, Katrina, had destroyed much of the South. E-mails began to arrive days later, describing the flooding, riots, and shootings. Stuck in the chaos of my own little world, I felt far removed from what was happening at home and could hardly comprehend it. For once, I understood what people must have felt when I wrote home about what was happening in Zimbabwe. I was left with a sense of detachment, being so far away and not knowing how to help.

September started off well, and through Project HOPE, Mai Chimbo and I were able to start five more women from the farms on income-generating projects. We gave them each a notebook to keep records of their progress each time they bought and sold items. Melissa had taught the health-care workers how to do this in a training seminar she had held, and they had passed the information on to their clients. Each of the women was HIV positive and already had some major health problems, so some of the health-care workers, including our good friend Mai Maposa from Peplow farm, offered to assist them with their projects. Mai Maposa did her work with so much joy that it rubbed off on us. Just as I was about to hit my frustration level for the day, she would always turn and say with her beautiful Shona accent, "You're doing a good job. Keep it up." That little bit of encouragement always lasted me a long time.

It also helped that we were beginning to see progress in some of the children who were HIV positive. Some of them had been placed on a special diet and were beginning to experience improved health because of these minor changes. It was so great to see them running around with renewed energy and big smiles, and I was learning a lot in the process.

Three good friends soon arrived for a visit, including Emily, who had earlier lived with me in Zimbabwe, and two other members of the FOSA board (now changed to mean Fairfield Outreach and Sponsorship Association, since the orphanage was turned into children's homes). The night before they came, I went to visit the mother of house one, Mai Mari Jeni. She needed a listening ear. Inflation was beginning to get out of hand, and everyone was suffering. The mothers were working faithfully day after day to care for the children at Fairfield but were not exempt from the hardships the economic situation forced on them.

Mai Mari Jeni spoke passionately about the issue, and I could now see their side of the issue and could better advocate on their behalf. When the FOSA members arrived, they spent many hours listening and giving everyone a chance to voice their concerns. Sometimes just having someone care enough to listen to your problems can cut your worries in half, but the FOSA members went a step further and took action to help resolve many of the issues right away. This provided a bright ray of light for the workers at the children's homes, as they now felt validated in their concerns.

At the same time the FOSA board arrived, they brought along a girl named Julia, who would be staying with me for the following eight months. It was nice to have someone to share my house with again, and Julia became like a little sister to me. Julia was put to the test from the very first day she arrived, and she passed with flying colors. The first morning she awoke in our house, we found that a rat had spent the night eating through the big bag of goodies she had brought from the States. Watching all those half-eaten American foods being thrown into the trash can was almost too much to bear for both of us!

I taught Julia how to wash clothes in a bathtub, how to cook using only a hot plate, and how to endure numerous knocks on our door at any hour of the day or night. She also had to quickly get used to all the big spiders that were beginning to come out of hiding after the cold winter months. She very patiently attended church on the mission with me each Sunday, sometimes sitting up to three hours in the heat of the packed sanctuary, listening to a Shona sermon that neither one of us could understand. We always had at least two children on each of our laps or at our sides, who became heavier as they sank into sleep lulled by the heat.

Julia also had some very real and difficult experiences out in the farm villages during her first weeks. We went together to visit Baba Dozva at his home. This was the same man who months before had been in the hospital lamenting with Melissa and me about the current situation. He was now bedridden, as AIDS had overtaken his body, and his wife spent long hours caring for him. We tried to talk with him for a few minutes, sitting on tiny wooden benches that had been brought in for us.

Baba Dozva waited until his wife had gone outside to fetch some water before turning to us and saying with a haunted expression, "Do you know she has to change my diaper? I am a grown man, and my wife now has to change my diaper. Is that any way to live?" He was still staring at us, waiting for an answer, as his wife quietly reentered the room. We prayed with him and left, only to return a few days later with Mai Chimbo for his funeral.

When we arrived, the wooden box holding the body was set on top of two chairs in the middle of a cleared area. It was right outside the shack where Baba and Mai Dozva had lived together with their young son, Happymore. After going through the line of mourners to greet everyone, Mai Chimbo, Julia, and I stood under the shade of a tin overhang outside the wooden structure that served as their home and watched people file past for one last look at the deceased.

Mai Dozva passed by us, and I could see the long sickness and death of her husband had taken its toll on her body. She was so thin and her eyes hollow. She could not look at anyone and nearly fell over when she walked by her husband's casket for a final good-bye.

We then followed the funeral party past the shacks, down a steep incline, across a small stream, and back up the other side to where the tractor was waiting to carry the body to the graveside. We parked at the bottom of the mountain at Guy farm and climbed the all-too-familiar path to the graveside. As I reached the top and looked down the mounds of dirt in a nice straight line, I remembered my other friends who were also buried there.

I listened to the songs of the women, their feet pounding a steady rhythm on the ground. I watched as the men dug deeper and deeper into the ground, right beside the spot where they had buried Mai Domboka. Then they lowered the box made of wooden planks and began to fill in the hole. I did not like the feeling of familiarity those actions brought, and I was amazed that Julia handled the situation so well. At only eighteen years of age and having been in Zimbabwe for only a few weeks, she was experiencing sights I would not have been able to handle at that age, but she did it with much grace.

Julia's quick acclimation to the culture continued, as a few days later we went to visit the family of Tadiwa, who had been in our program the year before. They insisted we stay for dinner. In honor of the occasion, Tadiwa's aunt, Mai Mwoyo, went out to kill one of their three chickens. I was allowed to take the feathers off, to everyone's amazement, just as Linda had taught me when we took baby Janine *kumusha*. Mai Chimbo was given the honors of cutting it apart, and Julia and I both watched with a mixture of disgust and amazement as she took all the insides out.

We took turns attempting to stir the *sadza* in the big pot sitting over the fire in the small kitchen hut until the smoke almost overwhelmed us. As the guest of honor, Julia was handed a plate full of food, complete with a piece of chicken from which a small heart dangled. I recoiled as I saw it, but Julia seemed to take it in stride. She merely continued talking to Baba Mwoyo as she ate and even managed to finish her portion of *sadza*.

After dinner we all sang and prayed together. Mai Mwoyo gave a testimony, saying that she had been feeling down but now felt encouraged by our company. She told Julia the story of how people had treated her when she tried to take care of her nephew Tadiwa the year before. We all sat in amazement and listened as this woman continued to praise God for her circumstances and for His being beside her through difficult times. I was once again filled with gratitude that God had allowed me to learn from one of His saints.

It was now the middle of October, and Mai Chimbo requested that Julia and I come to her house to meet a ten-month-old baby, who, she said, was no bigger than the size of a newborn. Although I thought she must be exaggerating, we started walking down the dirt path toward her home. Upon entering Mai Chimbo's house, I realized that she had not embellished the facts at all.

The father was holding Tino, a miniature version of what a baby was supposed to look like. We looked at his health card and saw that he had been born in December the year before and currently weighed in at two and a half kilograms, roughly five and a half pounds. His father explained that the mother had become paralyzed on her right side during the birth and was not able to feed the baby. They had been feeding him watered-down porridge for the first ten months of his life.

We drove them back to the bottom of the mountain near where they lived and began the long walk to the top. On our way, Julia suggested that the two of us raise him until he was big enough to go home healthy. The parents eagerly agreed. Caring for the baby had put much strain on them because Baba waTino was not able to work with both the mother and baby to look after.

As soon as we arrived back at the mission, Mai Chimuka from next door rushed over with nappies and pins and showed us how to bathe Tino's tiny body in a little basin. She helped us cook porridge for him, and we made two little beds, one in my room and the other in Julia's. Julia stayed up for his feeding at eleven o'clock, and I got up with him at two and at five. After a while, I laid him next to me in the bed because he wouldn't stop crying.

The next morning, we realized that we were now instantly a part of the community. People were visiting, helping, and laughing. People who had previously been afraid to come to my house because we were foreigners now felt free because there was a baby to visit. Even after one day, Tino seemed to improve, as everyone helped to move his arms and legs for his muscles to start working. Most of the time in his hut, he had just lain on the ground because his father was busy cooking or looking after the place, and his mother had been unable to pick him up because of her stroke. Tino started smiling at everyone, and the whole community embraced him.

Later that afternoon, however, Mr. Mufute and Cecilia called us into their office. They had spoken with social welfare, and Julia and I were not allowed to keep the baby because his parents were still alive. With much sadness, we loaded Tino's few belongings back into the car, and everyone lined up along the road to say good-bye as we took him back to his mother. We were able to deliver milk formula, wheat porridge, and peanut butter, along with some soaps and clothes, thanks to the donations that had been coming in the mail. We were also able to hire a girl to help care for mother and baby, which allowed the father to go in search of work. Returning that night, I felt a sense of sadness. Everyone had begun calling me Mai Tino (mother of Tino), and Julia was *Mainini* (little mother), the name given to the young sister of the mother. It had been nice to be a mother for a day.

I celebrated my twenty-eighth birthday that week with all the mothers from Fairfield and baby Janine as a special guest. We danced and sang late into the night, but my birthday gift did not arrive until a few weeks later. Every month that year from June through October, I had made the three-hour trek to Harare and smiled at the immigration officer as he informed me that yet another copy of some unimportant paper was missing from my file and I thus could not be issued a work visa. Then I would calmly call my mom and ask her to send another copy of the allegedly missing papers.

I think they were just waiting for me to snap, which is what I saw a lot of people do during my visits to immigration. They would end up screaming at the immigration officer until they finally stalked out of the room, only to return a few minutes later after cooling down. They knew that one officer held all the power in deciding whether they could stay in the country or would be deported.

One day in early November, a letter addressed to the administrator at Fairfield arrived. Baba Mufute called me to his office, and with a knowing look, he handed me the paper and stated, "Well, it looks like you did it." Confusion turned to disbelief as I read through the official document and realized that not only had my work visa been approved, but they had also given me two years instead of the usual one-year term!

Hugging the paper tightly as if it might disappear at any moment, I ran straight to house one, where Mai Mari Jeni was feeding her children lunch. I sat down beside her on the blanket she had spread on the kitchen floor and handed her the paper. This woman had prayed for my visa since the time I had arrived. When she finally understood that I had been approved, she jumped up, and the children joined us as we shouted for joy.

At that moment, I remembered my prayer so many months before: "Lord, if it is Your will for me to stay, make it impossible for me to go. If it is Your will for me to go, make it impossible for me to stay." As I looked at my friend dancing around the kitchen and at the children laughing and dancing with her, I knew the decision had been made. At that moment, it would have been impossible for me to leave in the midst of so much joy.

Chapter 13

Believing in Miracles

Miracles happen to those who believe in them.
— Bernard Berenson
American art critic

I soon started taking closer notice of the children at Fairfield who had tested HIV positive. We now had nine altogether, and I had come to know them quite well. There was Michael, who had a laugh that was infectious, especially when he started laughing really hard with his brother, Matthew. Another boy, David, on days when he was feeling good, would snap his hands down at his sides, smile showing both upper and lower teeth while squeezing his eyes shut, and then march around the playground until he knew you had noticed him.

Then there was Chenai, whose eyes lit up as he ran full force down the walkway from his house, huge smile plastered on his face, ready to give us all hugs. When I picked him up, he would gently pat my back and repeat, "I love you," head nodding back and forth rhythmically until he fell back laughing. I think he liked the English words coming out of his own month, merely strange sounds to a two-year-old who knew only Shona. Sara, on her rare moments of outgoing personality, would excitedly shriek my name over and over while holding her arms open wide, ready to be picked up. Rutendo had the most sparkling, beautiful eyes, and her baby smile seemed to steal the heart of anyone who noticed her.

These were my children now, and I loved them. I could only wonder when they would be taken from me and prayed that I would not take my time with them for granted. I sometimes became scared that something would happen to them, as I remembered other friends who had already suffered and been taken away by the disease. Each time I prayed, though, I could sense God saying, "Stay" or "Keep going."

One particular morning I sensed these words: "Don't give up. Love completely. Love people for Me in My name until it is done." I realized it was better for my children to feel loved while they were on earth and for them to show love in return than to hold them at a distance for fear they would someday disappear. God gave me the strength to do that. I realize now I could not have done it on my own.

There was still a huge stigma for people who were HIV positive, and some of the staff at Fairfield understandably felt it was better to keep the children sheltered from this for as long as possible. Michael was the only one who had started ARVs, but a few of the others were also starting to decline in health. It was painful to see them getting sick, and finally I was given permission to take two more through the long process of being registered for medicines at Mutare General Hospital. David, who had become one of my best buddies, and three-year-old Sara were chosen to go next because of their failing health.

This time the mother from house eight, Mai Chipidza, accompanied me so she would know the procedure. I was now prepared to sit in hospital lines for five to six hours at a time and thought I was equipped with at least a basic knowledge of how Mutare General operated. It turned out that this didn't do us much good, since the rules were ever-changing, and it seemed like whichever line we chose was the wrong one.

We woke very early on hospital mornings, arriving in the queue by six. As we waited hours for our hospital card to be stamped, David and Sara would sit patiently on the *zambia* (a piece of cloth that wraps around a woman's skirt) that Mai Chipidza had brought for them. David was usually all dressed up, with his shirt tucked in and his pants pulled up high on his waist, playing little travel games while Sara attempted to color pictures. They were the only two children in a sea of adults. I was always amazed to see how well behaved they were all day long, usually without having much to eat. There was no whining or temper tantrums. They simply waited.

It took David longer to get through the entire process of registration than it had Michael. This proved a lot more dangerous for his health, as we discovered David had a lot fewer soldiers fighting for him than Michael had. For a child to be started on ARVs their CD4 count (or number of soldiers) had to be at or below 15 percent. Michael had been right on the line with a CD4 count of two hundred. By the time David had his blood taken, his CD4 count had already dropped to 13 percent, placing him at a higher risk for infections. There continued to be complications as the months passed, and David underwent countless tests. The doctors wanted to wait for his body to be healthy enough to handle starting the new medicines without severe side effects.

In the meantime, we tried our best to help improve the children's health through alternative methods. Mai Chimbo taught Julia and me about the different herbs that could be used to boost the immune system, and we also started providing the children with fruit, peanut butter, and eggs to keep their weight up. It was very dangerous for an HIV-positive child to start losing weight, so this was the only line of defense until David could finally begin ARVs.

The children who were HIV positive at the children's homes began coming to our house on a regular basis to collect their extra food. Julia and I both loved David and began to look forward to his knocks on the door. He was always waiting outside with a big smile, wearing the gray knit hat we had given him to keep the cold out. Sometimes we would open the door to find no one, but the muffled snickering from behind his hand always gave him away, and we would find David hiding just around the corner.

It was at this point that I became an overprotective mother hen. I would find myself following David, Michael, and Matthew around all the time, saying things like, "It's cold outside . . . Where are your patter-patters (flip-flops)? . . . You need to be wearing a hat . . . Why are you coughing?"

I began worrying about them constantly, and this was most evidenced by what I like to refer to as the chicken pox incident. All someone had to do was mention that a few of the children at school had chicken pox and the whole of Fairfield Children's Homes was in a panic, convinced that the boys would catch it. We all remembered what had happened the last time chicken pox swept through the mission, taking Tsitsi, Learnmore, and Beatrice when they were still living at the old orphanage.

We all knew it was important to keep the HIV-positive children, with their already weakened immune systems, clear of these kinds of outbreaks. David, Michael, and Matthew were the only ones old enough to attend school, so the staff decided to keep them at home. Julia and I were happy to spend some quality time with the boys while the other Fairfield children were at school. In fact, it was during this particular week that the miracle happened.

David had become very sick during the first part of November. It had now been over two months since we began the process of trying to start him on ARVs, and the doctor had still not been able to start David on his pills. After a few weeks of our attempts to register, David started getting sick. He was turning into skin and bones, and I began to fear we were too late in starting him on ARVs.

Whereas before he had always had blood drawn without even flinching, now just getting a shot caused him great pain. When we took him to the mission hospital every morning and night for shots of antibiotics, he would scream and flail his arms, trying to get away. His health was deteriorating quickly, and he hadn't been able to go to school for about two weeks. The boy who could usually be found kicking the soccer ball with all his friends now stood sullenly on the sidelines, his little hat covering his head and his hands stuffed deep into his pockets.

Everyone at Fairfield was worried as we watched his body swell, his appetite disappear, and his cough increase. What worried me most was that my usually smiling, talkative little boy had quit speaking completely. We couldn't get him to say one word for over a week. One Friday the staff gathered in his room to pray. He no longer wanted to get out of bed. As we were leaving the house, I overheard some of the mothers saying that we all needed to fast and pray because God was going to heal David, but for the first time since meeting him, a dark fear began to creep up and take hold of me. That night I couldn't sleep. I was so afraid that something would happen to him, and by this time the possibility of losing him was too much for me to handle.

Around three in the morning, I decided to call my friend in the States. After listening to my long tearfilled story, my friend gave me an unusual piece of advice. Instead of allowing me to wallow any longer,

she challenged me to start reading three to five chapters of the Bible every day to see what God had to say. Looking back, I understand how wise she was to not offer me only human words of comfort, but also to remind me that my Father had a few words to say as well. I don't think anything else could have helped me during that darkest time of the night. What I came to were these words: "Do not let your hearts be troubled and do not be afraid" (John 14:27).

I had been filled with those two things: worry and fear. As I continued to read, I found that in the next chapter Jesus stated that if we remain in Him and His words, we can ask for whatever we wish and He will give it to us. I stared distinctly at the wall, and with what can only be described as a sliver of belief surrounded by a mountain of doubt, I said, "God, heal David." Almost immediately I fell sound asleep for the first time in weeks and woke an hour or so later to a knock at my door.

Dragging myself out of bed, I opened the door to find David standing there. As I stared in disbelief, he gave me one of those smiles I knew him best for, and he stepped into my front room.

"Can I have a drink? Will you cook me an egg? Can I have some peanut butter?"

I had almost forgotten the sound of his voice. I ushered him inside, willing at that point to give him anything he asked for. Later we took him to the doctor, and all he could say was, "Are you a miracle?" No one could believe what had happened. Over the next week, all of us at Fairfield watched amazed as he continued to improve, until one day his mother stood in devotions and said the words we had been waiting to hear: "Today I sent David to school."

God had heard us. God was faithful in answering, and every day as David continued to show up at my door, I became more and more grateful for the extra time God had given us to spend with him in good health. I would later hear stories of others on the mission who had been awakened that night and led to pray in faith for David to be healed. All those slivers of belief overcame the mountain of darkness that night and allowed God's healing to shine through.

A few weeks later, the Zimbabwean board for the children's homes met to discuss salary increases. This was the first time I was allowed to sit in on the board meeting. The mothers had not been given a raise in many months, even as inflation continued to spin out of control. The board finally decided on a 50 percent raise, but anything times nothing is still nothing, especially when inflation is threatening to top 1,000 percent. I was almost ashamed to tell them the news.

The next day at devotions, when the salaries were about to be announced, I was prepared to give a talk to cheer them up. Instead, Forward, one of the oldest boys at Fairfield, walked in and took his place where the devotion leader usually stood. As the thirteen-year-old spoke, there were no dry eyes in the room. He explained how he would be on the streets if it were not for the people in the room. He said that he would have never known what it felt like to have a mother if they had not been willing to work at the children's homes. He then opened his Bible and read about the five thousand people being fed and how God multiplied a little to increase the people's faith. I was amazed at what God did that day, as despite the meager salary increase, every mother and auntie stood up and went to work again. I had no doubt that their faithful service during those difficult times would someday be richly rewarded.

After a few months of living on our own, Julia and I welcomed a third roommate into the house in early December. During the evenings, Julia and Liz could be found making up dances in the living room or staying up to watch just one more episode of *Dawson's Creek* on the laptop. They helped remind me to relax and have fun in the middle of all the hectic days surrounding us. It was nice to have other people to help answer all the knocks at the door that started so early in the morning.

We were starting into the rainy season, however, and many different types of creatures tried to seek shelter in our house. I ran out of the kitchen one day to Julia's screams, as she tried again and again to flush the toad that had found its way into our toilet. Another day found both Julia and I on top of our dining room chairs as a rat ran right through the room and down the hallway. After we had spent a small fortune on rat killer, our unwelcome guest somehow ended up dead in our oven. Of course it took us a while to discover it, since we hardly ever cooked.

Our other "visitors" became many in number and usually ended up smashed under the broom we became proficient in using. Large spiders that could flatten themselves against the wall and move sideways at amazing speeds always made my heart jump with fear. Then there were the rain spiders that could actually jump. We had split up the household chores, and one of Liz's special duties was killing all the spiders. I actually think we let that count for two of her chores because Julia and I were so unwilling to do it.

One day in particular, a very large spider was crawling along the wall as Liz tried to smash it. With Julia and me screaming in the background, Liz continued to chase the spider with her broom. Julia, who had been diligently practicing her Shona, tried her best at using her new skills. Liz said, "I think I killed it."

Julia replied, "*Makorokoto!*" which means "congratulations." Then the spider resurrected itself and disappeared into our storage area. All of a sudden Julia burst out with "*Kupi* spider, *kupi* spider?" These were the correct words, just in backward order. She was actually shouting, "Spider where, spider where?" causing all the mothers a great deal of laughter when I repeated the story to them the next morning after devotions. I don't think Julia was thrilled to gain fame in this way, but she laughed right along with the rest of us.

We also became increasingly able to prepare for our frequent power outages that often led to the water being cut off. Each time we heard the refrigerator click back on, signifying the electricity had returned for a few precious hours, Liz, Julia, and I would run around plugging our computers and iPods in to recharge, filling water basins, and taking baths before everything went away again. It was a strange life, but I was very grateful to have two friends to laugh with through all the inconsistencies of living on the mission.

It was getting nearer to Christmas, and thanks to a donation from my church at home, we took all the children who had been in the top ten of their class to the movies and to pick out new school shoes. Lynn had come back to spend a few weeks with us, and the four of us made quite a happy household, wrapping gifts for all eighty children and preparing lots of surprises for our other friends on the mission and the surrounding areas. Eight of the twelve houses at Fairfield staffed with a mother and auntie was now at full capacity, each with ten children to share in the festivities. With the extra donations we received, we were also able to provide blankets, clothing, and school shoes to the children in the farm areas.

Our household woke up early on Christmas morning, and we experienced the joy of delivering the children's presents and placing them under the little trees they had cut down early in the morning. It was just like being Santa Claus, since the little ones were still asleep, but it was funny to think that none of them had ever heard of the man. In the afternoon, we went on a picnic and were given the best present of all. Our household grew that day as Shad and Abby, two tiny black-and-white kittens, came to live with us. Our family was now complete.

As the New Year started, we were able to get more organized and expand because of added funding. We placed ninety children in school under Project HOPE and began working on buying the material to have their uniforms made. I was constantly going back and forth between town, the mission, and the farms, trying to help orchestrate everything. I couldn't help thinking daily that I had the best job in the whole world. This was mixed at times by feeling overwhelmed and agitated by how much there was to do and how little difference all our efforts seemed to make.

God continued to teach me throughout that time about perseverance, patience, and love, while allowing me to work alongside some amazing men and women. It helped to remember back as we celebrated Tendai's fourth birthday that year. Here was the little boy who had almost died at three months of age happily blowing out his birthday candles. A few days later, Michael celebrated his fourteenth birthday, which was no small miracle considering how sick he had been a few months earlier. Now that he had started the ARVs, he was healthy and strong. When he stood up to give his birthday speech, he wished for many more years. Looking at him through proud tears, I finally realized his wish might come true.

Chapter 14

Caregivers

Religion that God our Father accepts as
pure and faultless is this:
to look after orphans and widows in their
distress and to keep oneself from being
polluted by the world.
—James 1:27

Over the next few months, many people in the HOPE program became very ill because of a lack of food. We had to increase our emergency food distribution to the most extreme cases. There was one woman in particular, named Mary, whom we had been assisting. She was an HIV-positive widow and good friend of ours. She had become very ill over the last month and we went to visit her at the hospital. I was instantly shocked at how thin she had become.

We had a long history with Mary and her three children. When I first arrived in 2004, Mary was still strong and healthy, always trying to find jobs to help her support her children. Now she was a mere skeleton, a shadow of the woman I remembered. I knew her white-blood-cell soldiers must have been disappearing quickly.

The day after she was released from the hospital, we went to visit her at Guy farm. She had to pull herself over to the doorway of her hut because she had become too weak to stand. While sitting on the stoop outside, Liz, Julia, and I listened as she told us that her relatives were no longer coming to visit her. Neighbors were telling her three small children that she was going to die soon. We held her hand as she cried, asking us who was going to take care of her children when she was gone.

No one should have to carry these burdens alone. Mary and her family needed the support of family, friends, and others in the same situation. This became apparent as we watched Mary in her lonely battle, her body beginning to deteriorate.

A few days later, we heard that Mary was in the hospital again. A few of the mothers from the children's homes went with us to visit her. Mary could no longer see and would talk about things that didn't make sense. She asked if she could drive my car and if Liz would play volleyball with her.

Mary also told the nurse that day that she wanted me to make all the decisions about her children. She had convinced herself that none of her family would take them. We had found that paranoia was common when people were going into the last stages of the disease. We later discovered Mary had a sister who was willing to look after the children, which provided us with much relief.

Mary was transferred that week to Mutare General in town and admitted into the infamous female ward A. This was the ward for women who were not expected to come out alive. We had heard many horror stories about nurses not carrying out doctor's instructions. There was limited medication available in the hospital, and they knew many people could not pay. The doctors made rounds only every few days because there were now very few doctors left in the country. With the economy continuing to plummet, many with a good education and job skills were trying to leave for more developed countries.

In response to all this, nurses often waited to follow the doctor's instructions until right before he was about to return. They didn't want to waste the medications if the person was going to die anyway. This may have been just hearsay, but every day we went to visit Mary, one of the women to her left or right had died the night before. They also kept the windows open to let the cold night air relieve some of the smell from the patients. Each patient was left to huddle under the one thin blanket given to them upon arrival at the ward.

Mary begged us to take her out of there. She said they were going to let her die, and she would rather die at home. Liz took her back to her hut that weekend, but it was a battle for her to even get Mary released. The nurses said she first needed to be started on ARVs, but no one was making any move to get her through that process.

Within a few days, it was evident to us that Mary needed to be taken back to the hospital. Her sister was not able to care for her because she had become so ill. We knew she did not want to go back to Mutare General, and the nurses at the Old Mutare clinic on the mission were far more caring. I arrived at Guy farm at dusk with Mai Chimbo, and we entered the little hut lit only by a candle. Together with Mary's sister, we laid Mary carefully on a folded blanket and then pulled it tight to act as a stretcher. She was only skin and bones now, so between the three of us, we gently lifted her and carried her up the incline to the road where my car was waiting.

As soon as we took her into the hospital, the nurses said she could not be admitted. She was now considered home-based care, meaning there was nothing more the hospital staff could do for her. We sat Mary in one of the wheelchairs, and her entire body folded forward, no longer able to stay upright. As they wheeled her into the medication room to give her a shot to make her more comfortable, I fell against the wall in the hallway and broke down sobbing. I had never felt so defeated.

We once more took Mary home, carrying her now under the arms and by her feet back inside her hut. We checked on her three sleeping children and assured the health-care worker, Baba Mlambo, that she would sleep well now from the medication she had been given. As we tucked her in, I put my hand over Mary's and looked into her eyes to see an eerily familiar sight. It was a dullness and fear that I had seen in so many other hollowed eyes in the past few years. Mary said her heart was broken and that she was going to die. It was at that moment that I knew we had lost. I gave her over to God that night and knew that although her earthly body was about to realize defeat, God was still holding on to her soul. "Fight for Mary," I whispered that night. "Take her safely home."

The next day one of the head nurses came to speak with me. "I heard you were turned away last night," she said. "Please don't be upset; it's only that there is nothing else medically we can do for Mary." It seemed they too had given up the fight for her.

I tried one more time. "We just want someone to help her sister care for her. The burden is too much for her on her own," I said. Finally, they agreed, and Mary rested that night under a nurse's watchful eye. She continued to deteriorate, and a few days later when I went to see her, she was outside, lying face-down directly on the grass. When I lifted the heavy blanket covering her, she blinked a few times.

"I'm blind now," she said. "I can no longer see you, but I know your voice."

I sat and talked with her for a few minutes, but it was clear that her mind was not completely coherent. As is common with many AIDS patients we visited, her health seemed to go up and down like a steep roller coaster, leaving us with sparks of hope for recovery. Mary followed this pattern, and the very last day I visited her before leaving for America, she was back in her bed, talking with me plainly and able to see again.

I sat on a small bench beside her, looking into her hollowed-out eyes, saying all the encouraging things I could think of, and promising she would never be alone. God was there with her even when we couldn't be. I knew as I looked at her that it would be the last time I would see her. I promised we would all work together to look after her children and that it was okay to rest.

As I walked from the hospital that day, I remembered two things that Mary had said to me during the time we had been friends. She once thanked us for helping people, and when I said that we hadn't really given her anything material, she responded, "You came to visit us when we were sick." I realized that day that the time we take to love people far outlasts anything we provide for them materially. The second lesson I remembered from Mary was something she said when we first met. We had been visiting together on the stoop of her hut, and she said she wanted me to give her a pair of trousers someday. I was surprised because most women on the farms were culturally expected to wear dresses and skirts.

"Aren't you worried about what people will say?" I asked her that day.

She replied, "Someday people will have to learn that it doesn't matter what a person wears. It's only what is on the inside that counts."

As I looked at her that day years before, I knew she was a woman I needed to know better. It does not matter the station we are given in life, because we all have something to learn from one another; and Mary taught me some valuable lessons I would hold with me for the rest of my life.

It was now time for Julia to return to America to start college. She had grown a lot during her time in Zimbabwe and had been a big help with the programs as well as a great encouragement to me. I was traveling back with her to visit friends and family for a few weeks, while Liz was staying in Zimbabwe to take care of Mary and the others. The excitement I felt about going home slowly began to overshadow everything else. As I flew into Chicago O'Hare Airport and weaved my way through customs, the man behind the counter asked how long I had been away. "Too long," I replied with a smile.

He handed back my passport and said the words I had been longing to hear: "Welcome home, Miss Roberts." I was home.

When I finally arrived in Columbus, two hours early, I was exhausted but determined not to miss the first glimpse of my family. I sat opposite the escalator and stared at it, my eyes barely blinking until my dad, mom, and brother popped up onto the platform in front of me. I ran toward them, dropping my bags to the floor, and as we embraced, I felt all my stress and tension disappear. It was a true gift to be home, although I could not stop the nagging thought that I should be helping Liz back in Zimbabwe.

Toward the middle of my trip home, I received a message from Liz asking if I could please pray for David because he had been taken to the hospital. I knew David routinely went in and out of the hospital all the time, but he always recovered. I was more concerned about the e-mail I received from Liz on May 16. "I'm sorry to have to tell you this over e-mail," Liz said, "but Mary passed away today."

Although many of us had handed Mary over to God when we saw her deteriorated state, I later found out that Liz never did. She continued to visit Mary daily and pushed for her to receive the ARV medication that had helped boost the immune systems of countless other people we worked with. Even after finding out that Mary had a CD4 count of one (she had one lone soldier left floating around in her body trying to stave off infections), Liz persisted, convincing doctors and hospital staff to at least try to save this woman's life. She never gave up on Mary, and her dedication taught me so much about perseverance and advocacy.

In the months and years to come, Liz would speak out on behalf of Mary to convince the world that if changes were made, people could have hope for their future. By doing this, she was able to keep Mary's memory alive, giving purpose to the life of a woman who had suffered silently through the system.

Chapter 15

Perseverance

*Will we give up? No. We must keep on going
because we have someone beside us and
inside us that has already conquered fear,
death, and disease. We will keep going
because we know that in spite of everything
that is happening around us,
we have already won!*
—Janine Roberts

B ack on the other side of the world, I continued
visiting friends and family, but Liz's messages
kept coming. Each time she became more insistent
that David was not doing well. "David has been
taken to Mutare General Hospital . . . "David has
been admitted" . . . "He has a high temperature and
is vomiting" . . . "David was just now having convulsions. He wouldn't stop shaking, and I am so scared
for him. Please pray for him."

By this point I knew what was happening. It felt like I was trapped inside a spinning cyclone and there was no way out. I remembered how Nicole had described Tsitsi's convulsions back in 2002, and the accounts were too similar. In the next-to-last text message, Liz told me that David had been diagnosed with meningitis and rushed in an ambulance to the government hospital in Harare.

My mind flashed back to when I had first met David. It was at the end of my first six-month term in 2004. I had been told that a new child had come to Fairfield and been immediately admitted to the mission hospital. I knew as I walked toward the children's ward for a visit that I should not expect the ball of energy that usually described other eight-year-olds I had encountered.

Instead, I saw a small boy covered from head to toe with scabies. He looked solemnly up at me from his bed and refused to speak, but something about him made me know we would have a special relationship, despite the initial meeting. I was just happy that he had somehow found his way here, as I watched his new housemother, Mai Chipidza, bring in a bucket of heated water to help him bathe. Afterward, he stood naked and shivering, as she patiently patted him dry and placed medicine on his wounds.

I soon found out that this was probably the first time in a long time that he had experienced a mother's touch. David had been discovered in the capital city of Harare just a few days earlier when his stepmother had taken him to the social-welfare office. His mother had died long before, leaving her disease to live on with her son. David arrived at the children's homes, complete with a paper stating his HIV-positive status. Now that his father had died as well, his stepmother, already in the throes of the disease herself, claimed she was no longer able to take care of him.

After David had spent a few days under the watchful eyes of the nurses, I found him sitting outside on the steps leading into the hospital. He was looking much better and enjoying the sun. I sat down beside him and pulled out a small green car made of plastic. Handing it to him, I saw the first hint of a smile, the first in a line of unending smiles and laughter that would follow during our friendship. He ran the car up and down the red clay stairs, looking up at me with a mischievous grin every few laps.

By the time I returned with Melissa that June, David was growing, happy, and healthy. We discovered that David was very bright in school, always taking one of the top positions in his class each term. He had been in and out of the hospital but, for the most part, was enjoying his life at the children's homes. Already he had managed to make friends with every child who came in contact with him. His funny laugh was contagious, and by the end of June 2005, Melissa and I had decided that together we would sponsor David. At that time he remained one of the only children who did not have any sponsors. There had been a hesitation to find sponsors quickly, since he had been so sick upon his arrival at Fairfield.

Just after Melissa completed her two-month stay and returned to the States for school that year, David celebrated his ninth birthday, together with his nine

Fairfield brothers and sisters and Mai Chipidza in house eight. What a difference I saw as I entered the party to find a beaming birthday boy in place of the former deteriorating child! I had found a small toy cell phone for him that instantly placed him at the receiving end of envy from all the other children. It made sounds as he pushed the buttons, phoning each of us in turn.

By August he was back in the hospital, continuing the ebb-and-flow quality of life common in HIV-positive patients. I read books with him every few days so his mother could go home to bathe and see her other children at Fairfield. David and I would lie on the little hospital bed together and read about all the funny creatures Dr. Seuss had invented. We also read about Spot and all the adventures of the little puppy.

David's times of health were getting shorter and farther apart, so the administration at Fairfield decided it was time to take David for registration at the general hospital in town. He was our second boy, after Michael, to begin the long process of registering at the OI clinic. I remembered all those days of watching with Mai Chipidza as he patiently played with Sara, waiting his turn to see the doctor.

The week David had stayed home with Michael and Matthew to avoid the chicken pox epidemic, we had all made pancakes together. David would get so excited when I flipped the pancakes, always exclaiming, "Oh!" like it was the most amazing thing he had ever seen. David loved going on trips outside of the mission. Luckily for him, a group from Africa University took the children on a group outing the previous December to see the beautiful waterfalls in Nyanga about an hour away.

When Julia, Liz, and I decided to take all the children in the top ten of their class to the movies that same month, David begged to go. He had gone with us every term prior to that, since he always did well in school. This time, however, he had come in at number eleven in his class after missing so many days when he was sick. All the children at Fairfield, who were usually very quick to point out who could and could not go on the top ten outings and firm in their decisions, unanimously decided that David should also be allowed to go. It made my heart swell with pride to see how they all rallied around and supported him.

David worked extra hard the next term from January to April and was rewarded by being placed back on the top ten list. He was also rewarded by finally being allowed to commence his ARV treatments. It seemed like everything was going in his favor, although he was very upset with me when he found out one of his doctor's appointments was on the same day as the prize-giving ceremony at school where he was to be one of the recipients. I think he had a hard time forgiving me for that, believing I had full control over the timings of his appointments.

All these memories flashed through my head over and over that week in May as I received each of the text messages from Liz describing the rapid progression of his illness. Then on Thursday, the first day of June, as I was sitting in a Chinese restaurant with my brother on his lunch hour, I saw my phone flashing. As I looked at the screen, I realized it was an international call—and I knew. I hit the button to silence the ringing and dropped the phone into my bag, unanswered. A little while later, I was driving to my doctor's office to get my malaria medicine for the return trip to Zimbabwe. My phone beeped to signal a message had been received from Liz, and I saw these words across the screen of my phone: "Trying to get through. Call as soon as possible—important."

I went into the doctor's office and signed the appointment book. I sat down on the edge of a chair, my movements slow and methodical. I stared down at the phone for what seemed like a long time, and suddenly it was ringing again. I knew I couldn't ignore it forever. My selfishness was causing Liz to suffer alone on the other side of the world. I walked outside into the sunshine and around the corner of the building, pushed the button to answer, and listened as my heart broke and shattered on the hard concrete of the parking lot.

Thousands of miles away, my baby had suffered, looking at someone else with questioning eyes, wondering why he was forced to endure so much pain. Thousands of miles away, I had sat laughing with friends, watching television, and shopping at the mall, left to wonder why I hadn't been there to hold him. I wanted to fly there right then, but there was nothing more I could do. I phoned Melissa, and her first words were, "You don't have to say it. I already know."

That Sunday I stood before my home church, and they allowed me to grieve as I gave a short eulogy, with Melissa sitting in the front row for support. We put David's picture on the altar, along with a single white rose in a vase with a pale blue ribbon tied around it. At the same time I spoke, on the other side of the world, hundreds of children lined the dirt road leading from the children's homes to the place where David's body was taken. They stood in complete silence as his tiny coffin was taken to its resting place. Grown men cried, stories were remembered, and David danced into the arms of his Savior.

After I was done talking, one of the members of our church came up and said her young son had listened to the story about David and said afterwards, "Mom, God really does answer prayers." God had used David even after he was gone to increase the faith of a little boy thousands of miles away.

A few months later, I would be sitting in Mai Chimbo's house when Mai Mashiri stopped in to visit after school. She said all the preschool children from Fairfield had been found in the graveyard that day, halfway up the mountain that surrounds the mission. They were running through the forest yelling, "David, David, come out and play." Their mothers had told them David went into the forest to live, thinking they were too young to understand what had happened. It made me smile a little to think that after all these months, even young children remembered David. I knew then that he had lived with great perseverance and joy through times of great suffering. He had made an impact on every life he had touched.

My heart healed just a little bit that day, and I knew that God was in the process of making it stronger, stitched with the love David had given me, so that I would be able to pass it on to others like him who didn't yet know they could be loved. Instead of thinking that I had the toughest job in the whole world, I remembered God had given me the best one. He was allowing me to help prepare His children to go home to His kingdom with peace, dignity, and love. I had to count on His promises and know that He would take care of the rest. I knew someday I would have to release David completely, but it would be a long, hard process, and fortunately, it didn't have to be done right away. Right then I needed to keep a piece of him with me.

Nine days after David's death, I returned to Zimbabwe, a little broken. There was a void that could be felt at Fairfield. David had touched every one of us. One of the aunts from his house came to say she was sorry about David. She said every day when they called the children in for dinner, they all kept asking, "Where are the others?" because it just felt like someone was missing. I could feel something heavy pressing down on my chest. I felt fragile, but I knew that if I could just cling to God, He would protect me. I also tried to cling to the people who brought me joy in Zimbabwe: Michael, turning as he pushed his wheelbarrow down the road, lighting up with the smile he was famous for; the mothers, singing with everything that was inside them at morning devotions; my friends and their visits in the evenings; and the children, falling asleep on my lap.

We returned to Mary's house to visit her children. Liz and I stood on the spot where they were building a new and bigger hut to accommodate Mary's sister and her children, along with Mary's three. I knew Mary would be happy to see them all laughing and playing together. God was there in the aftermath and was rebuilding and renewing this fractured family. As we said good-bye and turned to go, I knew we could all trust Him to do just that.

Liz returned home that week after a year of very dedicated care to the children at Fairfield and the families on the farms. I was sad to see her go, but I also knew that after all she had experienced with David and Mary the last month, she deserved a much-needed rest. I would find out in the coming months that she would have nothing to do with rest, fiercely determined to change the situation she had seen in Zimbabwe.

I woke from a dream shortly after Liz left, sure that I had seen Mary's face coming through a cloud of light, smiling and motioning for me to come with her. I took her hand, noticing that she was wearing the trousers she had always asked for, and we peered through the clouds. There I could see David running and laughing with other children. He turned, waved, and then also motioned for me to come, as Mary had. I realized I was a little girl again, as I took his hand and ran into the light, laughing and ready to play. For an instant after I awakened, I felt pure joy radiating around me. I knew with certainty that David and Mary were at peace and that I would see them again one day.

Chapter 16

Life Goes On

Do not live a grey existence that knows
neither victory nor defeat.

—Anonymous

The next few weeks, I was thrown into a hectic schedule, as a container arrived from the States. These large containers were at times delivered to the mission, sent with items needed for all the different groups. This one, which was for Fairfield and Project HOPE, had come mostly full of items that we could not find in Zimbabwe or were too expensive for us to buy. In what used to be Julia's room, boxes were now packed from floor to ceiling. Inside was everything needed to run the project for months. Among the treasured possessions were stacks of milk formula for the eighteen orphaned babies HOPE now cared for, clothing, school shoes, books, toys, and medications.

Fortunately, there was a mission team from South Carolina there that week that immediately set to work on sorting the boxes. They may never realize how much they helped us in just a few days, but if I had been forced to do the task alone, I would have been too overwhelmed to know where to begin. Our friend Lynn was back for two weeks and prepared us an excellent meal while we worked.

On one of the days when the team came to help, I received word that a mother had just died at the hospital, leaving behind a three-month-old baby and other children as well. Within a few minutes, the grandmother and sister, Ketai, appeared at our door, carrying the baby. Her name was Liberty.

In the midst of all the frenzied activity in my house, we were able to sit with these two women and pray as they wept over the death of this daughter, sister, and mother. As we did, two men from the South Carolina team were searching through the piles for what we needed: baby milk, baby bottles, and clothing for the child. One of the men lifted the old *ambuya* gently onto the bed of the truck that was waiting outside to take them back to Guy farm. Both mother and daughter smiled a little as Lynn handed them a small pair of booties and a hat sent by her friend. God was able to use every person on that team for a specific purpose that day. I felt blessed to have them by my side.

Shortly after, a woman showed up at Mai Chimbo's house one afternoon with her young son, Prince. The matron from the hospital had directed her to Project HOPE, thinking we could help. Her son had a heart condition in which not enough blood was exiting the heart, thus causing it to enlarge. If he didn't receive an operation in the next few months, his heart would explode. She explained to us that if the operation could be performed in Zimbabwe, social welfare would cover the entire amount. Unfortunately, all the heart doctors specializing in the area needed for this operation had already left the country. Prince would have to travel to South Africa to receive medical treatment, of which none of the amount would be covered. The mother was appealing to us for an amount close to three thousand U.S. dollars, and it broke my heart to tell her there was virtually no way we could come up with that much money so quickly.

Prince had to go for a review with the doctor at the end of June, and in faith we told her to book the surgery as soon as possible after that. I didn't even know who to ask for help with that amount of money, so we decided instead to ask people to pray for guidance. The first group I asked was my mission organization, CornerStone International. They prayed faithfully for each of their missionaries weekly, as well as for any specific requests we had. I wrote asking for prayers for this young boy, and by the end of the week, there was a response waiting in my inbox.

During their prayer session, one woman had stood up, walked to her pocketbook, and wrote out a check for the entire amount of the surgery. She said she felt God was asking her to be more obedient with her finances, and the result was this: Prince would have a new heart and a new chance at life. By the time the mother returned with her son a few weeks later, we were able to tell her to prepare her travel documents. Prince was going to South Africa. As God continued working in these ways, I could only be faithful in giving Him the glory by telling others what He was doing.

A few weeks later, Melissa returned for a month's stay. On our way back from the airport, we visited one of the mothers from Fairfield, a woman named Presca. She had been transferred to a hospital in Harare recently after two unsuccessful operations at Mutare General to remove stomach cancer. It seemed the cancer was growing too fast. Melissa and I laid gentle hands on Presca's bloated stomach as we prayed for her that day with her mom and other relatives surrounding us. Her skin was pulled so tight that it felt like she was pregnant. Her body had become very thin over the last weeks, since she was rarely able to eat anything.

Presca had been coming to my house for the last year on a regular basis, asking for Tums to help her upset stomach. Finally, the doctor, thinking maybe the problem was bigger than they had first suspected, had sent her for tests at Mutare General. With only a handful of qualified doctors left in Zimbabwe, Presca was forced to wait in the hospital week after week for the operation she desperately needed.

Each Thursday they would prep her for surgery and place her in a line with other patients. The doctor would come in and perform as many surgeries as he could for the day, and everyone else was sent back to the ward to wait another week. On the third try,

Presca was finally operated on. A large part of the cancer was removed from her stomach.

Assuming Presca's family would not have the funds to cover the private medical expenses, the hospital had sent her sample to the government lab for testing instead of to a private company. We knew this could mean the difference between life and death. Samples sent to the government labs usually disappeared, never to be heard from again until it was too late, while the private labs could return results within a few days.

She had been discharged a few days later, and I had picked her up at the back of the hospital, watching her frail body, still in her nightgown, shuffle slowly to the car. I remembered all the hard work she had done at Fairfield, first as a volunteer in the preschool, where she had worked long hours for free. Seeing her dedication, the administration had promoted her to aunt and finally to mother at the children's homes.

She would always come to my house on her way home from work, asking if I would read an essay she had written, practicing for her exams. She was trying to teach herself English so she could receive her high school diploma. Often she would ask for books to borrow and read. She had asked for one during this stint in the hospital as well but never felt well enough to read it.

Presca had managed to stay at home only a few days before being transferred to Harare, where I saw her with Melissa. It was unsettling to know that only two months before, David had been racked with pain in this same hospital only one floor below where I was standing right then.

Melissa and I returned to Old Mutare that same day and would soon find out that this year's visit would prove no less heartbreaking than the drama she had experienced the year before. During her last visit, Melissa had seen homes being burned down, experienced fuel shortages that affected every aspect of our work, and met children, like David, who would not be there to greet her when she arrived this time.

Within four days of her arrival, we attended a Bible study at the Meikles' house. Everyone was excited about Melissa's return. We were driving home when my phone rang. Melissa answered, and I watched as her face registered shock.

"What?" she exclaimed disbelievingly into the phone. "What happened? Was she even sick?"

Bracing myself for the news that was about to come, I asked Melissa, "Who is it?" never expecting the response I received.

"Mai Maposa," she said despairingly, as she stared straight ahead.

My reaction matched that of Melissa's. Out of the ten health-care workers we worked most closely with, Mai Maposa had been one of our best. She was always dedicated to her job. We had spent countless hours working alongside her to visit those in need at Peplow farm, where she worked. She was an honest woman who worked tirelessly to ensure that the sick and orphaned in her areas were well cared for and loved. Now she had suddenly been taken from us with no warning.

I realized that no one was safe here. Even those who appeared perfectly healthy could be taken in an instant. I remembered the last time I had seen Mai Maposa, only days before. She had been smiling and happy under her beautiful sun hat, as she brought the babies from her village to receive their monthly milk formula from Mai Chimbo's house.

The next day, along with Mai Chimbo, we went to help Mai Maposa's family with the funeral arrangements. Everyone, including her four children and all the orphaned children she had been caring for, were in a state of shock. We brought the white material that would be sewn into a gown and a pillow for her head. As I looked around the yard surrounding her hut, I noticed many members from HOPE whom she had worked so tirelessly to assist. Their lives had been changed because of her dedication, and some had traveled long distances to pay their last respects. I felt like everything was crumbling down around me and didn't know what to do.

Melissa and I left the mission that day to visit a friend in the rural areas for the weekend. It was nice to laugh with friends and have a break, cooking over a fire under the stars at night, but we were not prepared for what awaited us upon our return. We arrived at Fairfield around four o'clock that Sunday afternoon, only three days after the news of Mai Maposa, to find all the mothers gathered outside my house. As Cecilia turned toward my car, her eyes met mine, and I knew something was wrong.

"Someone has died," I told Melissa, only hoping I was wrong.

All the mothers walked toward us, and Cecilia, the obvious spokesperson, said, "Presca has just died."

My heart sank, my body following as it slumped over. She had fought so hard. The day I had taken her to Mutare General, her tears had fallen, worrying about what any mother would worry about when she knows she is dying: "Who is going to take care of my son, Janine? He doesn't even have a sweater for school, and it is cold. Who is going to take care of my son?"

Her words echoed in my mind now as we all started walking toward her house to pay our respects to her relatives. Together with all the mothers from Fairfield, we went down the receiving line, hugging and consoling Presca's family, including her sister Sophia who sat engulfed on a black couch that had been placed outside the house. She looked lost. Presca's young son wandered around the yard, not knowing what to make of all the commotion. I remembered my promise to Presca that day in the hospital that I would help take care of her son. We all would.

Now we stood silently. After a while, we all went inside the house and sang. Many of the younger women would stay all night to sing, a traditional way to make sure that the family was not left alone to grieve but would be lifted up by the presence of others. Some of us left a few hours later and passed through the hospital. One of Fairfield's gardeners, Dzawanda, had been admitted and was very ill. We were all coming together as a community because of the tragedies that were happening, and I felt blessed to be a part of the support system.

The very next morning, Melissa and I were in town to arrange for Presca's funeral. We had to wait a few days for the funeral, as the body was being transported to her rural home and her mother and other relatives had to find transport to get there as well. While we were running our errands in town, I received a phone call from Cecilia that one of the Fairfield children had suddenly passed away after an episode from epilepsy. Mildred had been transferred from Fairfield just a few months earlier to a place that could better assist with some of her problems. Now the administrator from her new home had phoned to say that when they had tried to wake Mildred up that morning, they discovered that she had suffocated sometime in the night during one of her epileptic seizures.

I remembered when I met Mildred in 1998 on my first trip to Zimbabwe. She was just over a year old, wearing her little pink skirt and sweater. Her curiosity and playfulness touched the hearts of those who knew her, and having her body so far away placed an extra burden of stress on the mother she had lived with at Fairfield as she made plans to go to her funeral.

Melissa and I traveled the next day with the others from the mission to Presca's rural home. We left on the school truck early in the morning, crammed into what looked like a large cage fitted onto the back of the truck bed. There were about fifty of us, all covered with pieces of cloth or jackets to keep the dust from getting in our hair and eyes and on our clothes as we traveled.

When we finally arrived after a few hours of bumpy driving, I opened my eyes to a very dry, flat piece of land with only one house in view. This had been Presca's rural home, and we all filed inside one of the huts, singing and clapping. Everyone took turns paying respects to Presca's mother. She sat on the floor with her legs straight out in front of her, her arms hugging desperately a thin wooden box beside her: Presca's coffin. She wailed and pointed to the coffin with desperation as I arrived on my knees next to her and held her tightly.

Presca had been a prayer warrior for many and taught me a lot about serving others with humility and gratitude. Her funeral lasted from morning until dusk, as people continued one after the other giving testimony to the life she had lived. Linda, Fairfield's secretary, was asked to be the master of ceremonies. The opening song was *"Hakuna Zita Kunga Jesu,"* or "There Is No Other Name but Jesus." Presca had asked us to sing that song to her the day before she was transferred to Harare. I was happy it was being sung now as they brought Presca's body out for final viewing.

As the younger women danced and sang outside the hut, pounding the ground with their feet, the people carrying the coffin laid the box on top of two chairs. Opening the top of the box, someone pulled the white cloth down from Presca's face revealing just one eye and a small part of her face. Two girls held white cloth over the coffin in order to block the sun, and someone else waved a feather like a fan over Presca's head. People began filing past, and when it came time for her sister Sophia to have her last glimpse, she wailed and fainted to the ground. We all followed a truck that took Presca to the burial site, and I wondered if this family would ever recover from the loss they were experiencing.

Part of my answer came quickly, and the rest would come during the months that followed. As the sun was going down and we were loading back onto the truck bed, I turned to see Sophia going to collect water with her cousin. Fading into the sunset, I could see them laughing happily, and I knew everything would be okay. God had already begun a healing work, and time would heal the rest.

After a few weeks, Presca's mother returned from the rural area where she had stayed to mourn the loss of her daughter. She showed up late one afternoon with Sophia and Presca's son. They had come to thank Melissa and me for helping and brought a live chicken to show their appreciation. I knew that it was a very extravagant gift for them to offer, but what meant the most were the words Mai Chapotoka spoke or, rather, sang.

She knelt down on the ground and began praising God, and then she said God had given her a song to sing to us. I could no longer see through my tears, as this woman who barely spoke a word of English took hold of my hand and began singing clearly, "God will take care of you, through every day, o'er all the way. God will take care of you. God will take care of you." As I watched this woman sing so earnestly,

I remembered that God really had been taking care of me all this time and that He would continue to do so.

Chapter 17

Love at First Sight

*Hope is necessary in every condition. The
miseries of poverty, sickness, and captivity
would, without this comfort,
be insupportable.*

—Samuel Johnson
From Laura Moncur's
"Motivational Quotations"

Afew weeks later, Melissa and I were still recovering from all that had happened. It was July 31, David's birthday. A year ago to the day, I had been sitting in his living room, surrounded by his mother and nine brothers and sisters at Fairfield as they sang "Happy Birthday." That year Melissa and I had bought him, along with his coveted toy cell phone, a little shirt with chickens on it that he wore when we went on hospital visits.

This year, to celebrate his life, Melissa and I traveled to one of the farms for the day and passed out clothing to other children in need. God really helped me to release David a little more that night. Just before going to bed, I sensed very clearly these words: "I have him. He is here with me. He is not suffering anymore. He served his purpose, and now he is resting. I have him." I was not used to hearing so much from God all at once, but I felt such a peace that He had spoken these words to me. It was comforting to know that David had a specific purpose and that God was able to fulfill it through him. God had seen his bravery, and now he was able to rest.

As we moved into August, Melissa's time was nearing an end. We had been able to have some fun adventures in between all the hardships. We drove to Nyanga and hiked out to see beautiful waterfalls plummeting so far that they disappeared into the distant water below. We carefully maneuvered our way down the large rocks to a place near the mouth of the falls where we could sit and look over the vast view of the land below us.

We also were invited by Jane Keis to visit the hot springs a few hours from our house one day, swimming in ponds and pools warmed like bath water by the springs that filled them. We had even been able to run (or rather, walk) at a not-so-fast pace in a half marathon hosted by Africa University. Walking over Christmas Pass down into Mutare that day gave us such a unique perspective of the land around us, but seeing Mai Chimbo cross the finish line an hour after Melissa and me was the highlight of the race.

The week before Melissa was to leave, we went to the VCT to drop off some supplies. We had now started working with the VCT staff, since many of the clients from our HOPE programs were HIV positive. Sitting on a wooden bench outside their offices was a little girl named Karen, who immediately lit up when she saw me.

Something inside me loved her right away. I found out from the staff that she and her mother were being tested to find out their HIV status, and she was waiting outside for her results. The tiny eight-year-old immediately wanted me to sit beside her. She wanted to go to my house, ride in my car, and even asked her mother if she could live with me. Her bright smile contrasted greatly with her frail body.

Her mother had been walking a very long distance, carrying Karen on her back each morning to make sure she received her daily shots to fight the TB coursing through her body. The results came back: both mother and child were positive. Melissa and I drove them quietly to the bus stop that day, passing through our place first. Karen had only one simple request while she waited for us to gather some items for them. "*Ndinoda mvura,*" she said, asking for cold water.

I didn't see her for the next few days. It was soon time for Melissa to return to the States. While I was driving back from the airport, I received a call saying Karen was in the hospital. As I entered the children's ward, she stood up on her bed, spreading her arms wide in excitement. I hugged her gently, only now realizing just how tiny she really was. The first time I had seen her, she had been wearing sweat pants, but this time she wore a pale yellow dress, her skeleton-like frame exposed. I could see every bone in her legs. I could see the outline of every rib. Delicately lifting her onto my lap, I felt as though she might break at any minute. She eagerly asked to call her dad.

"I want to tell him to come see me," she said. "I want to tell him I am sick, so he will come." I loved her so much, as I watched her excited expressions.

The next night she went with her mother to the house of the VCT coordinator. Karen asked again for cold water, very cold water from a refrigerator. Not owning a refrigerator, the coordinator went to a next-door neighbor and returned with the water. As Karen drank, the coordinator talked to her. She asked, "Do you know who Jesus is?"

"No," the little girl replied.

"Jesus loves children, and He always stays with them when they are sick. Do you want to know Him? He loves you," she asked Karen.

Just before she fell asleep, Karen whispered back, "I love Jesus."

Two more days passed as we watched her physically deteriorate. When I looked into her eyes, there was the same look I had seen in the first man I met in the last stages of AIDS and everyone since then: the skin pulled back so tightly on the face that the teeth were exposed, the eyes so hollowed it seemed I could look right into the soul. Seeing Karen, I knew it was almost time for her to go. She no longer stood and smiled when I came into the room. When her mom tried to sit her up to eat, her head would drop back and her body would slump down.

Finally, she could not even respond to anyone. I visited her that morning to bring her porridge and then headed to the VCT to see a staff member. As we were buttering our bread to have tea, I looked outside and saw Karen's mother running out from the hospital, screaming. We knew that Karen must have died. Her mother collapsed on the ground, as our teacups and spoons crashed to the floor and we ran toward her. My friend and I brought her inside the hospital and into one of the private rooms.

While the nurses were talking to Mai Karen (mother of Karen) to make sure she was all right, out of the corner of my eye I saw two nurses standing over Karen, one male and one female. They tucked her in but didn't cover her head. It looked like I could just walk up and talk to her.

That's when I heard one of the nurses say, "She isn't dead. She's just sleeping. Go and see her."

I felt like laughing, as the crowd had laughed at Jesus when He told them the little girl was not dead but only asleep. As I walked toward the room where Karen lay, however, I could see a slight movement under the blankets. She was breathing. People slowly began to leave the room, where Mai Karen had shoved herself far underneath a bed. She lay sobbing facedown on the cement hospital floor. The nurses all tried to tell her that Karen was just sleeping, but she was adamant that they were lying. Karen had gone into convulsions just moments before, and when she lay still, her mother thought she had died.

Finally, she looked at me and said, "Sister Janine, is it true?"

I looked her in the eyes and said, "Your baby is alive. Go and be with her." She stood up, brushed herself off, and with a deep breath took her place again at the foot of her daughter's bed.

Karen improved a little throughout that day, able to eat some and a little more responsive. The TB drugs were weakening her little body as they fought the disease. When I left them that night, Karen's father had finally come and was setting up a mat so he could sleep on the floor next to her bed. By that point, she could hardly recognize him. Her mother lay down next to her, holding her closely.

The next morning I received a phone call from the VCT coordinator. Karen's mother said she had fallen into a deep sleep around one that morning. When she awoke, Karen had passed peacefully away. As I walked with the parents to get a ride back to their home, I remembered Karen asking for cold water. She always asked for cold water. When I told Melissa that Karen had passed away, she also mentioned this and reminded me of the following verse: "And if anyone gives even a cup of cold water to one of these little ones because he is my disciple, I tell you the truth, he will certainly not lose his reward" (Matt. 10:42).

I realized, then, that sometimes our purpose in life is to give others the opportunity to choose to do God's work. My little friend fulfilled this purpose. She shined with Jesus' light through her immediate and unconditional love and acceptance of us. We did nothing to deserve it. Then before going home, she allowed us to follow through with Jesus' simple request. We would not have had the opportunity to give her cold water unless she had asked. For this I would always remain grateful for our brief meeting.

*   *   *   *   *

Early one morning the following week, a young girl came to see me. Lisa was the daughter of one of my good friends from the farms, Mai Lisa (mother of Lisa). Lisa had been very ill lately and sent home from school with a large lump protruding from the back of her neck that closely resembled the one I had seen on Michael the year before. Lisa had also suffered severe weight loss, leaving me with only one conclusion.

No one seemed willing to talk to her about it. I explained to her mother that Lisa needed to get tested for HIV right away, since her condition might worsen quickly. Her mother said she had talked with her before, but Lisa had adamantly denied any activities that would cause her to contract the AIDS virus. Mai Lisa said she could not ask her daughter directly if she would have the test, but she asked if I would be willing to do it.

Now with Lisa sitting in front of me wondering why I had called her to my house, I was beginning to have second thoughts. What was I supposed to say to this thirteen-year-old girl without offending her that could possibly make her understand what she needed to do? Finally, I explained that many of the symptoms I had seen in my HIV-positive children I was now seeing in her. I told her I wanted the best for her and wondered if she would consider coming with me to be tested. She started to cry quietly in my living room that morning. Her mother had in fact found the courage to talk to her the night before. She said it would relieve her mother to know the truth and agreed to have the test done.

As she was standing to leave, I said, "Your mother was the one to convince you to have the test, and because you love her so much, you are willing to do something very brave in order to put her mind at ease. Now I want you to go back and have the same conversation with your mother. She also needs to be tested."

Many people who worked with HIV-positive patients had seen Lisa's mother drop in weight over the last months. They were very concerned and had tried on numerous occasions to convince her to be tested. Each time she would laugh it off and change the subject. Now, with Lisa's agreement, I knew she was the only person who could make her mother see the importance of being tested.

Mai Lisa came back to my house later that evening. She sat down, looked at me, and said, "You are a very clever girl," with a mischievous look in her eyes. It was settled. We were all going to town for testing on Monday. Lisa had done her job well.

I could see Mai Lisa was very worried and said to her, "Don't think too much. Let's just wait and see what the results will be."

Tears started coming down her face. "I am not worried about myself, but only about my daughter. Will she even be able to get married?"

She began singing *"Mwari Mubatsiri Wedu"* ("God Is Our Helper"). I sang along with her, each of the verses now very familiar to me, except one. At the end of the regular verses, Mai Lisa kept singing *"Ndinewe, ndinewe,"* which I had never heard before. She explained that the previous night she had awakened with these words running through her head. She felt compelled to get up and sing them for many hours. The words literally mean "I have you," or "I will be with you." Mai Lisa said she knew that God was preparing her for something. She had surrendered and waited. When I had asked her to come speak to me, she knew this was the situation for which God had prepared her.

That Monday morning, the three of us headed to the VCT for the testing. We discovered that since Lisa was a minor, she needed an accompanying letter from the doctor. I would have to bring her back the next day when Mai Lisa was at work. Mai Lisa, however, had made a promise to us. She went in to have the test, and when it was time to hear her results only a few minutes later, there was only a look of acceptance as a positive result was read.

The next day, Lisa and I returned to the clinic. Since she was under eighteen, the results were read to me alone in a closed room. Lisa would have to wait and hear the results directly from her mother that evening. As the paper was unfolded, I saw a miracle in the form of a tiny check made next to the word *negative*. As the realization washed over me, I felt immediate joy. Lisa had her life back. We had been wrong, but God had His plan the whole time. He knew the only person who could have convinced Mai Lisa to be tested was her daughter. Now, with the right medications, Mai Lisa's health would steadily improve and she could live for many more years. God had used the daughter to save the mother.

The beauty of it did not escape me that night as I entered their house to tell them the good news. The electricity had gone out, as it did so often in the evenings. Over the light of a small candle, I handed the results to Mai Lisa, with her daughter waiting expectantly in the doorway. She accepted it with trembling hands, and the immediate change in her expression told me she understood what the check on the paper meant. She and her daughter hugged and danced together in the candlelight, with Mai Lisa crying over and over again, "It's negative! Praise God! It's negative!"

Chapter 18

Small Reminders

There is a time for everything, and a season
for every activity under heaven: A time to be
born and a time to die . . . a time to mourn
and a time to dance.

—Ecclesiastes 3:1–4

Soon after, the Meikles, who had fought so long to keep the last bit of their land, were finally forced off their farm. Their family had been in the country for three generations and had suffered through many horrible tragedies during their lifetime in Zimbabwe. My Shona friends had also been through intense times of struggle. It seemed that the two colliding cultures of European and African descent had created much misunderstanding, leading to mistrust on both sides over the hundreds of years they had lived together.

I only wished that one day my Shona friends could understand and see the faithfulness of the

Meikles. It exemplified God's heart. I had also seen this same faith demonstrated by my Shona friends in the villages and at the mission. They shared God's heart as well.

Dave and Irene Meikle were once again threatened, and Mr. Meikle finally told them to stop. They could take the farm; he was not going to fight anymore. They had one day to remove all the belongings they had collected during more than thirty years of marriage and leave the property. Mr. Meikle's family had purchased the farm over a generation ago, but they would now leave behind the house, farm equipment, and anything else they could not collect by the following day. They would leave all this to the new owner, receiving absolutely no compensation. Days later the same thing would happen to the owner of Guy farm.

With the farms being resettled, they would no longer be as safe for us to visit. Home visits would quickly come to a halt, and soon we would have to depend on people coming to us if they needed assistance. As for our families living on the farms, their future was uncertain. They were now at the mercy of the new owners as to whether they would be allowed to stay in their huts on the property or would be sent away.

As I helped to unpack their belongings at their son's house, Mr. Meikle gave a complete recap from inside the farm during their moving day. The family was closely watched while they were packing to make sure nothing fixed to the house was taken, such as light fixtures or covers for electrical outlets. Mr.

Meikle asked if he could take the wooden toilet seat he had so lovingly given to his wife one Christmas. Even after a resounding no, Mr. Meikle was determined to have the last laugh in this very serious situation.

Just before they left with the last truck full of household items, Mr. Meikle said he had to use the toilet. As soon as he shut the door to the bathroom, he pulled out his miniature screwdriver, removed the wooden toilet seat, and with one swift motion tossed it out the window and into the bushes. Walking with a determined step, he went around the house, retrieved the seat, and buried it among other items packed in Larry and Jane Keis's van. It was quite a shock when the Keises found the toilet seat later as they unpacked, but Mr. Meikle had won that argument, shedding a little light on this otherwise dark day.

*   *   *   *   *

The following week, a man came into the Fairfield staff office. He said a woman had been chased the night before as she was going home from church. Although very pregnant, she managed to outrun the man who tried to attack her, but she was later rushed to Mutare General Hospital. She gave birth early, and the man who came to us was seeking assistance for her.

Since Mai Chimbo and I were already going to town that day, I stopped by the hospital to check on the woman. I managed to find the maternity wing, and asking directions from the nurse, I wove my way through the maze of hallways until I arrived at her room. The woman had given birth to a perfectly healthy baby boy and thanked us for coming to visit them. The new mother asked if there was a name I wanted to give the boy. I named him Joshua, in honor of my brother, who at that very moment was flying over the ocean to visit me.

I was so excited that my brother had decided to come and experience some of what I saw every day. During his short visit, I tried to fit in as many different experiences as possible. He met the Meikles and went golfing at Leopard Rock Hotel, one of the nicest courses in all Africa. Leopard Rock Hotel was a beautiful castlelike hotel on top of a tall mountain, with a slab of sheer rock jutting straight up behind it. The hotel was given its name because people used to hunt for leopards there long ago. Surrounding the hotel were the grounds where the golf course was laid out, each hole overlooking an increasingly spectacular view of the mountains into Mozambique.

The next day, the VCT coordinator and I drove with Josh to a place called Staplefold to try to find one of the babies on our milk program. It turned into an all-day event, stopping at Lake Alexander along the way, with its clear sparkling water like nothing I had ever seen. The landscape changed so drastically the farther we drove from Mutare, and eventually the air chilled. All around us were tall spiky fir trees covering the mountaintops.

For the next few days, I took Josh to places near the mission, including Guy farm. Mai Chimbo and I had decided that until we were told otherwise, we would still visit there. Josh met Faith, Mary's children, and even Dancing Grandmother, who, of course, brought out some of her best dancing skills. A few days later, we went with two friends, Richard and Phoebe, to Nyanga. About an hour from Old Mutare, we saw some of the same waterfalls Tiffany and I had toured during our trip in 1998.

That evening I stood singing and washing dishes at the sink with Phoebe at our cabin as Josh and Richard sat happily roasting marshmallows outside. I later joined them, staring into the bright flames escaping from the fire. I could feel the heat contrasting with the cool of the night air and wished my brother could stay longer. It had been so nice to have someone from my family experience what I lived every day.

Josh left a few days later, after a great time at Imire Safari Ranch where we got to ride on elephants through the open bush. Stepping off the high wooden platform and onto the elephant's back was one of the most daunting experiences I had ever had, but the majestic and graceful nature of the animal made the ride unforgettable.

When we finally arrived at the airport in Harare and Josh walked through the gate, a feeling of loneliness washed over me, and I suddenly felt so tired. I realized I wanted to be walking through the gates with him, onto the plane and out of this country that had been the setting for so much death and hurt in months past. I was scheduled to go home in a month to celebrate the Christmas season with my family, but it felt like years away as I watched Josh disappear toward his boarding gate.

I returned home to life on the mission, where God continued to send little reminders that although we were experiencing great suffering in Zimbabwe, there was also an abundance of joy and blessing. The morning after I said good-bye to my brother, I woke up early to the sound of children laughing and playing outside my window. They often used their water buckets to produce a steady drumbeat as they sang their morning songs. The children were the best alarm clock I could have ever asked for. Matthew sang made-up words at the top of his lungs as he waited his turn at my outside water tap. Mai Chimuka yelled from the kitchen, "*Ndiani?*" wanting to know who was making all the noise. It was quiet for a few minutes before the chatter started up again even louder than before, and it made me feel happy.

By eight o'clock, the entire staff of Fairfield Children's Homes was in the conference hut, ready to start devotions. My eyes were renewed to the beauty of all the mothers singing and dancing with everything that was inside them. Walking each morning into that room filled with the harmony of twenty-five African mothers who were shaking maracas and dancing had now permanently stamped itself in my memory. It would always remain one of my favorite experiences in Zimbabwe.

The women stood around me in the circular hut, voices raised in praise to God who was continuing to take care of them. Their faith continued to amaze me. Most of the mothers worked twenty-four hours a day caring for ten children who were not their own. They carried out their duties with a joy and diligence that could not be matched by even the highest-paid worker in the country. It was clear that these men and women were no longer working for man, but for a much higher purpose. I felt honored just to be in their presence.

After we left devotions that morning, about thirty of the children arrived at the playground behind the conference hut, ready to begin their day at crèche. Fortunately for me, they were given some extra exercise by running right past my house on their way to their classroom. That meant thirty hugs and thirty big smiles to start my day.

I jumped on my bicycle later and rode to Cidimu farm to visit some of my kids. As I passed the primary school, I heard a few young boys shouting, "*Murungu, murungu,*" meaning "white person." My heart faltered for a moment, disliking the phrase. A second later, I heard one of the children from Fairfield scolding the boys. "*Haasi murungu,*" he told them. "*Ndisisi Janine*": "That is not a white person. It is our Sister Janine." My face beamed.

After leaving Cidimu farm that day, I moved on to Guy farm. Children ran from their huts to play games with the soccer balls that had been sent to them a while back. Mountains with strange rock formations at the tops rose around me on all sides, creating the perfect backdrop as the sun set behind the tiny huts and turned them into beautiful shades of gold and orange. I knew these days were probably numbered; since Guy and Meikle farms had been taken over, the future of the orphans living there remained uncertain.

Although I knew the physical places where we worked would soon change, the nature of the work would always remain the same. Giving and receiving love was the best job description in the world, and I felt privileged and blessed that God had brought me to Africa. I finally began to realize that forming relationships with the people was far more important than "doing" and being busy all the time.

I decided to try to put this into practice for the last month before going home for Christmas. I made sure I was home every afternoon when the children finished school and set out two big boxes of books and games so they would feel welcome to stop by my house. Within a few days, my living-room carpet was covered with small children in their uniforms coming straight from school to enjoy coloring, reading, and puzzles.

Faith was one of the first to tentatively walk through the door. She was still terribly skinny, so this was also a chance to slip a little extra food to her each day. Mary's children came often and practiced reading to one another. Mary's son Adam came one day and slept on a little mat on my floor all day. He had been sent home from school sick and had nowhere else to go.

Most of the children were coming from Guy farm, which was understandable. There was a great sense on instability among the workers there since the farm had been taken. Many families that had been employed by Mr. Guy feared being forced to leave their huts. I hoped that coming to my house gave the children a few more hours of stability before going home to the chaos occurring there.

Apart from those coming from Guy, other children came regularly as well, including Judith. Judith came almost every day to ask if she could come live at Fairfield. She had been living at the mission hospital since her mom died there at the end of July. The police were still trying to track down any relatives, but in the meantime, Judith had been left sleeping on the hospital floor while her mother's body remained in the morgue for over four months.

Late one evening after school had started in August, I slipped into the hospital while Judith was sleeping on the hard floor and laid a uniform and shoes next to where her head rested on her arm. The headmaster had agreed to allow Judith to come to Hartzell Primary School at Old Mutare Mission until the social-welfare office found a place for her. At least that gave her something to do during the day.

It was now the end of October, and not much progress had been made concerning Judith's case. I was finally given papers to take to social welfare the day her mother's body was finally taken from the morgue. Since no relatives were located to pay for a funeral, Judith's mother had a pauper's burial. This meant a truck came and picked up her body, stapled a piece of plastic around her, and drove her to a mass grave, where she was dumped with five or six others who had reached the same fate. There was no marker to locate her. I couldn't imagine the pain Judith must have gone through without a proper way to say good-bye to her mom.

On the day the truck came to take her mother away, Judith showed up at my house with half a loaf of bread and a Freeze-it. With a big smile, she handed them to me before walking back to the hospital in her new school uniform. I was still standing in my doorway watching her go when Nyarai popped around the corner. She explained that one of the hospital nurses had given Judith money to buy a treat on this difficult day. Judith had gone straight to the little tuck shop by the school and spent all the money to buy the items I now held in my hand. I was deter-mined to make sure Judith had a safe place to live.

Taking her to the Fairfield administrator, Baba Mufute, I explained the story and asked if she could have a place at the children's homes. I tried my best to explain to Baba Mufute that if Judith could be given a chance in a real family setting, I was sure she would flourish. He instantly agreed, and Judith came to Fairfield on a temporary basis. One day she came into the administrator's office and said, "Thank you for letting me come here. I now have my own bed." Baba Mufute said at that moment he knew he had to give her a chance for a future. Judith would remain as one of our children until almost a year later when social welfare finally found her older sister, who was able to provide for Judith.

More good news came the following Friday when I was in town buying groceries for the HOPE chil-dren. Out of the eighty children at Fairfield, we had eight remaining who were HIV positive. Michael,

Rose, and Sara had already been through the registration process in town to start their AIDS medications, but I wanted to make sure the rest were started on the process. Two of them had found a special place in the hearts of many of us at Fairfield: Chenai and Rutendo.

Chenai was well on his way to three years old and attended preschool, but he had been brought to the children's homes just shortly after his birth, covered from head to toe with a rash no one could explain. At the very moment that Chenai was near death, a group from the States arrived, carrying a very strong antibiotic that the doctor immediately gave to the little boy. After two courses of the medicine, Chenai began to recover.

Rutendo was brought to the homes about a year later, malnourished after being abandoned in the bushes at birth. Only a few days old, no one expected her to live very long, but thanks to the care of the staff at Fairfield, she began to recover. Over the next few years, these two quickly became the favorites of anyone visiting the homes. Chenai and Rutendo would sit on the porch of house ten together and wait for any unsuspecting person to walk by and then start waddling down the brick pathway, arms stretched wide for a hug.

Now it was time to take the remaining five, including Rutendo and Chenai, to have blood samples taken to see if it was time to start their AIDS medications. To do this, they first had to be retested for HIV. In some rare cases, the result could change from positive to negative around eighteen months of age, because the mother's antibodies could still be in the baby's blood at birth. Just before taking the children to the clinic, I knelt in my bedroom, praying a one-sentence prayer: "God, please give us just one." I knew it would be a long shot, but if even one of the five tested negative, it would be a miracle.

After they were finished with the test, I went into town while awaiting the results. I sent a text message to the VCT coordinator, asking if any results had come back negative. The coordinator sent me back a message saying, "Three are negative; only two are positive." I literally started shouting in my car, all by myself, with lots of people walking by and looking at me. I couldn't believe it. Out of five children who tested HIV positive at birth, the chance of three now being negative was just not humanly possible. I had to find out who they were.

I phoned the coordinator, and she told me our little girl Alice was negative as well as Rutendo. As she began shuffling through her papers, I couldn't imagine who the third could be. All the rest already had many of the physical symptoms of the disease. When her voice came back on the line, I heard her say, "It's Chenai."

The first thing I did upon arriving back at the children's home that afternoon was enter house ten, where Rutendo and Chenai sat playing on the floor. Both of them came running out to greet me, and as I bent down to pick them up, scenes from their future suddenly flashed before me: Chenai on his wedding day and Rutendo graduating from high school. So much had been given back to them with the negative test results. They had been given a new lease on life, and at two and three years old, they didn't even realize it.

As I thought about these two, I realized how significant their names were to this journey they had started. In Shona many names signify the parents' feelings during the time of birth or perhaps something they hope the child will fulfill in life. Chenai's name means "to be made clean," or "to be made pure." God did this for Chenai. He made his body clean of the HIV infection. *Rutendo* in Shona means "faith," which was definitely present through the many people who had loved her and prayed for her to be healed.

For months to come, Rutendo and Chenai continued to sit on their porch, waiting for unsuspecting visitors to walk by. Chenai was now old enough to manage an all-out run toward a person before jumping into their open arms. The love they showed was joyful and immediate, the kind of love that Jesus wants us to mimic.

By taking all our sins to the cross with Him, Jesus gave every person a new lease on life, like what Chenai and Rutendo had been given. We were all given the chance to be made pure in a spiritual sense and to accept this free gift by faith. Now my response only needed to match that of Rutendo and Chenai: joyful and immediate love for God and every unsuspecting person who happened to walk past my porch.

Chapter 19

Realization

*Those who sow in tears will reap with
songs of joy.*

—Psalm 126:5

A few days later, I left for a retreat at Victoria Falls sponsored by a Christian organization in the States. Any missionary from the surrounding African countries was invited to a four-day retreat, where they had counseling sessions, devotions and singing, and time for rest. I felt my guard come down as soon as I stepped into the luxurious hotel and was handed a fluted glass filled with fresh mango juice. It was fun to watch the surprise on the doorman's face when I thanked him in Shona for helping with my bags.

I was shown to my room, where fresh sheets were already turned down on the bed and a beautiful view of the Zambezi River could be seen through the arched doorway that led to a private patio. I registered downstairs and was shown to a table in the dining room, which was full of friendly couples who had traveled all the way from the States just to prepare this special weekend for us. The next few days were filled with reading by the sparkling pool, hikes to the river, and great food.

We were each allowed one free activity, so I chose to go on the ultralight. This is basically a go cart with a tiny motor on the back and wings like a hang glider. As I stepped into the small contraption, the pilot turned and smiled, saying into his headset that I shouldn't worry, because this was his *second* time to fly over the falls!

Only after we were high in the air did he explain that he had been flying these machines for years. That made me feel slightly safer until we began to head straight over the massive falls from about fifteen hundred feet up. With air pushing past us on all sides, I felt like I was really flying. On the way back, we saw miniature elephants and hippos scattered across the ground. It was scary but peaceful, all at the same time.

Later, when it was time for my counseling session, the husband-and-wife team counselors asked me all about my children back at the orphanage. I described some of the deaths that had occurred throughout the past months. At the end, they presented me with a simple question, to which my answer surprised me greatly. They asked, "What do you really want?"

My immediate answer was, "I want to go home." I realized at that moment that I was so tired. God

234

had sustained me with positive experiences over the recent weeks, but the pain from the earlier months was still hidden just below the surface. That night I returned to my room to find letters from family and friends spread out across my bed, a surprise from the organization that had sponsored the retreat. As I opened one after another, God reconfirmed what I had told the counselors: I wanted to see my family. I wanted stability for a while.

The last card I opened that night was from my dad. He told me he was proud of me and that I was brave. That is something daughters need to hear from their dads. God had worked miracles over the last few years, and He had helped me to be brave through many situations. Being brave meant being obedient, no matter what God said to do. I would wait to make a permanent decision about leaving Zimbabwe after I had heard from Him, but for now I decided a short trip back to America was needed.

The mothers gathered on my porch about a month later, as they always did when any of us was going away on a journey. They sang and danced among good-bye hugs and promises to see each other soon. Even with this send-off, there had been too much heartache over the last months. I traveled home in late November with a heavy heart and lots of decisions to make.

For a few weeks, I gained strength from my family and from being separated from the worsening economic situation in Zimbabwe. Back in Zimbabwe, the deaths kept piling up while I was away. Mai Dozva, the woman who had helped care for her ailing husband just the year before, suddenly died from untreated malaria. Where would her son go? I remembered Mai Dozva's bright smile each time I visited her at Cidimu farm, where they grew roses for export. Every few weeks she would send a huge bouquet of multicolored roses to cheer my home. Her smile was planted firmly in my mind, and I would miss her.

Next, Mai Chimbo sent news of one of the nurses from Old Mutare Hospital. I had just attended a wedding with her and some friends before I left, and we had shared a lot of laughter together that day. Her granddaughter had not been able to wake her in the morning, and no one was able to tell what she had died from. Rosemary, one of the mothers in our HOPE program, also passed away, leaving her four children with no one to look after them.

The worst news came right before I was supposed to go back to Zimbabwe. Mai Chimbo herself became violently ill with cerebral malaria, which is extremely deadly. Instantly people from all over the United States who had worked with Mai Chimbo began sending funds and prayers. The last report we had from Zimbabwe was that Mai Chimbo was near death and not eating or responding to anyone.

I couldn't imagine what we would all do without her. She had always been the one who held our program together. She was the one who knew what to do and how to do it. I prepared myself for the worst and began to shut down my heart. I was not ready to leave my family and go back to where things were so incredibly difficult.

Fortunately, right before I left America, there was a board meeting at CornerStone, and they invited me to speak with them. I walked into the room where the board had convened, and the director simply said, "Share your heart with us." It all came out: the love I felt for my children as well as the difficulties I faced in Zimbabwe.

Scenes flashed through my mind of the past years and what we had all experienced together at Old Mutare. I saw the rows of graves and how small the mounds of dirt were when children were buried. I saw myself ducking awkwardly out of Mary's small hut as her sister and I tried to stretch the blanket tight enough so that it could act as a stretcher for her. I saw Mai Chimbo helping to lift the frail body of Mai Mberi onto the back of her thirteen-year-old daughter so she could go to the hospital. I saw the look of shame in Baba Dozva's eyes as he told us his wife had to change his diaper. David, Karen, Tadiwa . . . they all flashed through my mind and I felt overwhelmed. I felt like I was treading water, incapable of moving forward.

After I had finished speaking, the room was silent. A moment later, the director said he had asked one of the board members to pray that God would show him a picture to give to me for encouragement. The man looked at me and said, "I don't know much about you except what I have just heard you share, but this is what the Lord showed me for you this morning." He began to speak, and I could see the picture before me.

.w an orange, and I got the sense that the
was your heart. God took the orange and
peeling away the outer part and then pulled
the sections of the orange open. He then gently took
out three seeds from the center. He took them away to
a place where there were three small mounds of dirt,
and He planted one seed in each mound. He breathed
on each one and poured water on them, and then
there was darkness for a while. Finally, shoots started
coming out of the three mounds, and they continued
growing quickly until there were three orange trees
heavy with oranges.

"Then I saw many people coming from the villages
toward the trees. Many of them were women, and
they began filling their aprons with the oranges until
the aprons were full. They then turned and took the
oranges back to where they lived and began passing
out the oranges to everyone in the village.

"I get the sense that what God has sown from your
heart will bear fruit. What God has done through you
already will bear fruit."

As he spoke, my hope was renewed. We all
prayed together, and I heard God speak very clearly,
"I will make this right." All the doubt and feelings
of failure seemed to melt away as I remembered that
Zimbabwe and the people I loved there would never
be impacted by my efforts alone. What God set as
His purpose would be done, no matter how much I
tried or accomplished or failed.

Although I loved my friends in Zimbabwe, God
loved them more, and His will was going to be
accomplished through them. I knew what I had to do

now was grieve the loss of my children and friends, but it would take time. CornerStone agreed to pray with me about whether I was to stay in Zimbabwe. I did not want to leave Zimbabwe permanently until I knew for sure it was the next step God had for me.

On the same day that I bought my return ticket, I received word that Mai Chimbo had been seen sitting outside the hospital, talking to her friends. Not even twenty-four hours earlier, Mai Chimbo had been in such a horrible state that many people were afraid she was about to die. For all the people who had seen her at her worst, it was nothing short of a true miracle. God had completely healed Mai Chimbo within a number of hours. She later said there were days that she did not remember anything, but somewhere in her there was a sense that she had to pull through. For the sake of Mai Chimbo and my beautiful children waiting at Fairfield, I gathered my shreds of remaining strength and once again boarded the plane for my faraway home.

One major change upon my return was in my accommodations. I had known for a long time that I could not continue living on the mission with so many people coming to my house at all hours of the day and night. People would come to my door or window, insistently knocking until I answered, whether I was asleep, in the bath, or trying to cook a meal. Privacy did not exist for me.

My decision to move was solidified when my home on the mission was broken into while I was in America. It was my friend Linda's wedding day, and the entire staff and all the children from Fairfield had gone to the church for the celebration. Luckily, Nyarai had returned early to work in her backyard garden and heard someone inside. Yelling for the men, she ran back to the church, but by the time they returned, the thief had escaped.

I phoned the owner of some small cottages about a fifteen-minute drive from the mission. He said he had a little one-room cottage available for me to rent. When I arrived to see it, I knew that this was my new home for a time. Honeysuckle grew out front, and birds chirped softly from the surrounding trees. That first evening I was back, a friend came and walked with me in the gardens that were all around the grounds. I knew I needed to enjoy the blessings that were around me. I had missed the simplicity while I was away. As we walked, I prayed that God would help me live for each day and trust for the future.

This proved to be a difficult task, considering that everything seemed to go wrong that first month back. It seemed I was being tested, and I fumbled and faltered my way through each day. My car broke down time after time. Electricity went out when my chicken was only halfway cooked. My phone wouldn't call out or receive calls, and I got my bags a week late from the airport and with many items stolen. When I unlocked the door to my old house to see the damage done by the thief, I found the place overcome with frogs. I was reminded of the plagues that Pharaoh dealt with in the Bible. Frogs were coming out of the toilets, sitting in empty buckets and trash cans, and hiding in closets.

It seemed that anything that could go wrong did, and I felt myself pushing and fighting in an endless battle. Something wasn't right anymore. I had always felt a very specific sense of purpose while in Zimbabwe, and even on the hardest days, I had an overwhelming sense of joy and peace. Now, however, everything seemed nearly impossible to handle.

That month Ketai passed away. She was the last remaining daughter of an old *ambuya* living at Guy farm. They had been the two who came to my house the year before with three-month-old Liberty, the tiny infant desperate for milk after her mother passed away. Fortunately, a container filled with infant formula had just arrived from the States. Liberty was assisted right away, and the family had gone home to mourn the loss of their daughter.

From that time on, the aunt and grandmother took care of nine children, all under the age of ten. Three were the aunt's own children, and the rest were orphans from all her sisters and brothers who had passed away. Now Ketai had also passed away. She had been very ill but was forced to work long hours to get enough money to feed the large family of children. Now the grandmother was alone, bent under the weight of carrying Liberty on her back. There was no way for her to get food for the children.

By the time we heard about the situation, the grandmother had disappeared with the children. Since the farms had been taken, our visits there had become less and less frequent. With this urgent need, however, Mai Chimbo and I set off for Guy farm. We finally found Dancing Grandmother, who was able to give us some information. She said a man had come and driven the children and grandmother far away to a place where they might be able to live and get some donated food. We didn't know where they were or if they were actually being given any food. After losing all her own children and now with the burden of nine grandchildren to look after, I knew this granny, with Liberty strapped to her back, was feeling very afraid.

We decided to use our old channels of communication, although they were quickly disintegrating. I contacted Baba Mlambo, the faithful health-care worker for Guy farm, who agreed to check on the whereabouts of the family. About one month later, the old granny showed up at Fairfield one morning with five grandchildren in tow, including Liberty. She explained that they were now going to stay with her niece on another nearby farm.

Together we carried bags of mealie-meal for making *sadza*, and loaded them into the trunk of my car. The children and granny all piled in, and we made one stop at her old hut to collect the other children. We drove all the way to their new home, where joyous relatives welcomed them. Each took a bag of mealie-meal, and I stood at my car and watched one, two, three, four, five, six, seven, eight, nine children disappear happily into the woods, ready to start their new life with granny. My work here was done. I felt satisfied, like something was finished.

During that month, I could not get the book of Isaiah out of my head. One peaceful Saturday morning, I opened my Bible to sit down and read it. The first words I read were from chapter forty. I immediately put the book down, and uncontrollable sobbing and a sense of relief overtook me: "Comfort, comfort my people," says your God. "Speak tenderly to Jerusalem, and proclaim to her that her hard service has been completed." (Isaiah 40:1)

As the tears flowed, I felt the largest weight being taken off me and all the tension and stress disappear. Every time I had thought about leaving Zimbabwe, I was so afraid to disappoint God. With this one verse, He had given me permission to rest. I couldn't have handled anything else at that point, and God's grace covered me.

Although the next month would be filled with ups and downs of clarity and confusion, the idea slowly became confirmed in my mind. I soon had an overwhelming sense that I was to leave Zimbabwe. For now, I was to prepare to go so that when it was time, I would be ready. I couldn't help but think what an amazing assignment God had given me over the last few years.

There was only one thing holding me back: I felt I owed it to Mai Chimbo to stay. She had always been so dedicated to the work we did together and wanted to see it become something that would last. I went to her office one day and explained how I had been feeling. When I was done, she looked at me and simply stated, "Janine, I am tired too. Maybe God will give someone else this responsibility for a while. For now, let's call it a day."

We were finished for now. We laughed together and clapped hands in the traditional Shona way. I knew now I could truly begin to release the responsibility that had lain so heavily on me for so long.

Later that week, I was hiking up a mountain with a friend. We were looking out over the city of Mutare, which had been my home for the last two and a half years. I told him I was confused because I really felt like God had told me it was time to prepare to leave, but not where I was going next. My friend said that if I had nowhere specific to go, I should go home. We can be in service to God anywhere in the world, my friend explained, so if He hadn't specifically directed me somewhere, it was best to be near family and friends who supported me. Going home seemed too good to be true. Could this really be what was next for me?

Chapter 20

Full Circle

God, grant me the serenity to accept the things I cannot change, the courage to change the things I can, and the wisdom to know the difference.
— Reinhold Niebuhr
The Essential Reinhold Niebuhr: Selected Essays and Addresses

A change began to occur as I increasingly felt assurance that it was time to leave. I wanted to leave the children from the HOPE programs in the care of people I trusted. I began turning over the programs to the Fairfield administration, Baba Mufute, Cecilia, and Linda. They each agreed to do part of the job so that the children in the farm areas could receive their school fees, medical care, and nutritional assistance. Cecilia had helped others who came before me with this type of emergency outreach, so she had some great ideas from the very beginning about how the program could run smoothly and benefit those in the most need. It was a great relief to know my children would be well cared for when I went away.

We did not know during those peaceful days at the mission that chaos was about to break loose in Zimbabwe. The atmosphere in the country suddenly changed when one Sunday that March, there were uprisings in Harare. For months the government had banned any large gathering of citizens. The opposition party had knowingly broken this ban by holding a prayer rally to pray for change in the country. As the main leaders of the opposition approached the stadium where the meeting was being held, they were attacked and taken to the police station.

The next day riots broke out in the high-density areas of the capital, the same areas where I had slept peacefully just two years earlier when visiting with my friend Rumbidzai. On Tuesday the riots hit Mutare, although they were short-lived. Army vehicles moved in to control any situations that might arise, and it became common to see soldiers with weapons standing at every corner in town.

The director from CornerStone contacted me, asking that I go to South Africa to wait for the violence to settle down. I was glad that the HOPE programs were now safely under the care of the Fairfield administration and began making plans to leave. God had prepared me just in time. From that point on, Zimbabwe began to spiral out of control.

We mostly experienced turmoil through the increased exchange rate. Just a few months before, the numbers had become so high that cash registers could no longer register them. Within a few weeks, all the old currency had to be taken to the banks and new currency issued, removing the last three zeros from all money and everything we purchased. For instance, an item in the store that had cost Zim$1million now cost Zim$1,000. This sent people into a confused panic all across the country.

Within just a few weeks, any of the old money still in circulation was useless. Even at the new rate, the parallel market was selling Zim$5,000 for US$1. By the end of the week, the rate rose to 8,000 to 1. Gas prices increased at the same time, although most people's salaries stayed the same. One week later, the exchange rate doubled to 16,000 to 1. By the end of the month, the rate hit an all-time high of 27,000 to 1.

The mothers at the orphanage were still earning the 120,000 Zim dollars allotted to them in a February salary increase, meaning that they were caring for ten orphans twenty-four hours a day on a little over four U.S. dollars a month. Meanwhile, some people continued to increase their wealth through the illegal sale of diamonds that had recently been discovered in our area. Mansions were being built, new cars were brought in from South Africa, and the gap between the poor and the rich increased. There was no more middle class in Zimbabwe. A person could buy everything, or he could buy nothing.

As all this happened, roadblocks into the city were put up immediately in an attempt to stop the diamonds from being illegally transported outside the country. Police were trying to curb the trade in smuggled gems that was costing Zimbabwe millions and millions of U.S. dollars. Roadblocks had been common throughout the years I was in Zimbabwe. Sometimes they were set up to search for weapons or simply to stop carloads of people who might want to start riots in the city. Other times the police were searching for illegal goods brought in from Mozambique. Generally, if I was polite, they let me pass with no hassles, but now there was hostility in the air that scared me each time my car was stopped.

I felt very fortunate to be getting out of the country for a while, especially in the middle of so much chaos and rumors that the airports might soon be closing as well. South Africa sounded a lot more stable, but I worried about my children. The mission was usually the safest place someone could be if any political problems broke out, but lately the government's party had been holding big meetings on the mission's grounds.

Just before I left for South Africa, I came into devotions late one morning to see everyone looking somber. Something bad had happened. With my limited Shona, I heard them talking about Dzawanda, our gardener at Fairfield. He had been in the hospital for a long time, and I knew as I began hearing the words "funeral policy" and "*chema*" that there was only one conclusion: Dzawanda, the strong, quiet man who had always worked so hard for the children, had passed away. He was the one who had carried each tiny coffin to its resting place every time a child passed away at Fairfield.

Now we waited all day until a much larger coffin arrived. All the mothers filed to the mission morgue, and we sang unending hymns as his wife wept. Forward, one of our boys at Fairfield, had always had a special friendship with Dzawanda. I was speechless as I watched Forward climb into the back of the truck bed and help to pull Dzawanda's coffin inside. I walked back down the hill afterwards, with my arm around him as he wiped back his tears.

At the same time, Dzawanda's mother was sitting in her hut in the rural area, awaiting her son's body. She would weep and throw herself on it, asking why Dzawanda left no children behind for her to see his face in. Life felt so unfair at that moment, and I could only cling to the fact that God had promised justice in the end. Otherwise, nothing we were experiencing made any sense at all.

I left that next week, arriving safely in South Africa, where Ron and Joanna Zeiner, also missionaries with CornerStone, enveloped me with the kind of hospitality that showed they had lived in Africa for many years. They instantly became my surrogate parents for the month. I slept for the first time in weeks. There had been many nights in Zimbabwe when I had awakened in a panic. Now, so far away, my fears seemed unreasonable.

One of my first nights in South Africa, I made a list of all the close friends and children I had lost since the previous year. When I finished counting, the final number was fourteen. They had died so close together that I had stopped mourning them. In the safety of the Zeiners' house, I began to allow myself to grieve. Each night before I went to sleep, I chose one person from my list and remembered them well. I thought about fun times we had together. I asked forgiveness for times I should have treated them better. I wept for them, and I released them back to the Father, one by one.

When I finished, I would close my eyes and God would give me a very special gift. I could see Jesus waiting for them, and I would hug each one and watch them walk into Jesus' open arms. The most beautiful was Karen. She had been a skeletal frame by the time I met her. Now, as she walked toward Jesus, her body was filled out to the size of a normal, healthy little girl, and she was wearing her yellow sundress. That was the only person He let run back to me for one last hug before they left together.

Finally, I breathed a sigh of relief as I finished the list. God lifted the heavy weight of sorrow I had clung to for so many months and replaced it with His comforting assurance. I again felt release and certainty that it was time for me to go home.

I returned to Zimbabwe for exactly ten days, just long enough to pack my belongings and say good-bye to the people I loved so much. There was a now a sense of urgency on my part, as emotionally I could not reenter the mind-set it took to live in such hardship. The political situation had not improved, and safety presented the second impending reason for my necessity to leave quickly.

Those were the hardest days I have ever experienced. So many factors had gone into my decision to leave, and I had been processing them for many months. Most of the people on the mission, however, were shocked with disbelief as I fumbled through explanations as to why I had to leave so quickly.

I entered devotions my second morning, and through tears that streamed freely down my face, I announced my decision to the entire staff of Fairfield. I looked around the room, remembering parties, children acting out plays, and mothers singing music that went straight to my very soul. The next morning I repeated this rite to the nurses, staff, and patients at Old Mutare Hospital. My knees almost collapsed underneath me as the staff said their heartfelt good-byes, and scenes flashed across my memory: sitting with David by candlelight while he waited for his shots, the room where Karen reached up in her little yellow dress to cling to me, and the bed where Baba waBenji said his last words to his son.

Mai Chapotoka was one of the nurses at devotions that morning. She and I had enjoyed a close relationship since her daughter Presca had passed away the previous year. After I made my announcement that morning, she left work and began making preparations for a very special surprise. In midafternoon I was called to her home, along with our friend Mai Keisi, where a feast was spread out before us. There was rice, *sadza,* chicken, vegetables, and even two bottles of Coke. Realizing that she must have spent her entire monthly salary or more to afford such extravagance, I was overwhelmed by her generosity.

This served as my only good-bye party in Zimbabwe, but it meant much more to me than any big fanfare. Mai Keisi, Mai Chapotoka, and I danced, ate, sang, and prayed with each other through tears of mutual gratitude for what God had given us.

The last two weeks, I stayed with the Meikles, whose generosity could never be truly repaid. They fed me hot meals each night when I returned from a wearying day at the mission, with Mrs. Meikle speaking her kind and quiet words of assurance. On the outside, I moved through those few days like a robot performing duties I knew I had to complete. Inside, my heart had already broken into many pieces, held together now only by sheer will, for fear all of me would fall apart entirely. I just wanted the pain to be over.

I spent as much extra time as I could with my children. I read to them. I hugged them and told them how proud they made me. I told them I loved them and that God did too, and even if I had to go, God would be right there with them.

On my last day, as I finished packing the last few items left at the mission house, Nyarai and Moses joined the many children who now came regularly to sit on my floor to play games or read books. I was going through my purse and handed Nyarai the half-filled container of Tic Tacs that I had. I looked up just in time to see Nyarai pouring the contents into her hand and giving half to Moses. I smiled as my mind flashed back to nearly ten years before, and I realized we had now come full circle.

A five-year-old Nyarai was splitting her Lifesaver in two and placing half in her friend Moses' mouth as tears stained his cheeks. They were sitting in the outside courtyard of an old orphanage that reeked of urine and resonated with cries that no one answered. Now the two teenagers sat side by side on my couch, well dressed, well fed, and well educated. They laughed and told stories until it was time to return to their separate houses, where their mothers were calling them in for dinner.

I was sure there would be more hard times in store for Zimbabwe and more ups and downs in my own life. I didn't have all the answers or know what the future held, but seeing Moses and Nyarai, I knew one thing would remain constant: God was still with us. He had been there from the beginning and would continue loving us and walking with us, wherever our paths led.

I boarded the plane for home, not ready to face reality. I went straight to my parents' house, and the next month went by quickly. I was given that sacred time to recover a little, and my parents gave me the space I needed to just exist. After a while, though, the questions started going through my mind. What was I supposed to do now? Feelings of failure overcame me, and I was sure that I had abandoned my children. The day my plane landed in America, the Zimbabwean government had made all shops cut their prices in half to try to stop inflation, causing many to close overnight because they couldn't afford new inventory. There was now little food available in the country.

After five weeks or so, I began traveling to see friends, but I felt strange and out of place, the first signs of reverse culture shock setting in. I remembered my professor from seminary saying that once we claimed another culture in our hearts, we could never again feel 100 percent normal in our own culture. I now knew firsthand what it felt like to be in surroundings I grew up in but yet feel like I didn't completely belong.

I tried to forget about Zimbabwe, but flashbacks became progressive. I didn't talk much with God, but once during that month, I thought I heard Him. It was a humid night, and the whir of the air conditioner kicked on in my second-floor childhood bedroom just as I was about to drift into sleep.

I asked into the darkness, "What do You want me to do now?"

I sensed the words, "We're going home," and I saw in my mind a picture of the city where I had attended seminary. I didn't really trust my listening skills at that time, but two weeks later I felt it confirmed. CornerStone held their second board meeting of the year in July, and I traveled to Kentucky to speak to them once again. They had been working for months to create a three-month reentry program for missionaries when they came back to the States. They asked if I would like to attend, and I immediately accepted. By the end of August, I was moved back into the quiet town of Wilmore, Kentucky, just a few blocks from where I had lived for three years of seminary.

During those three months, I was given the space to reconnect with God. He spoke so many beautiful words to me during that time, many of which I tucked into my heart and mind to sustain me for the future. He continued the healing process from all the pain of grief I had buried deep inside.

One day in particular, I saw myself in an ocean during a storm. The waves were coming up over me, and I struggled to catch my breath and stay afloat. I felt God with me, but I was afraid that I might drown, so I begged Him to put me on the beach. Immediately I was there, with my legs hugged close to my chest and my hair dripping wet, sitting next to Jesus, who was on my left. Instead of feeling relieved, however, I felt guilty and alone. I looked out at the storm and the waves and imagined my friends from Zimbabwe still in the midst of the storm. I had abandoned them there.

I opened my eyes for a moment and asked to see the truth in this situation. Again my mind was drawn to the beach. I looked out toward the storm again, but then my head turned to the right and saw the shoreline spread in an arch beyond me. They were all there! Every one of my Zimbabwean children and friends dotted the shoreline, safe and smiling. God had rescued all who asked. The physical circumstances in Zimbabwe were still the same, but He rescued us in the midst of the storm and set us on the beach where we were safe and protected, even if all around the physical world was still spinning in chaos.

I realized over those next few months what a truly precious gift I had been given, to experience and know Zimbabwe in a way that few others ever would. God's grace is always sufficient for us, and as I remembered people in so much pain and suffering from AIDS, I knew His grace had been poured out on them in such a measure that it was almost tangible.

I had the privilege to stand beside that grace, to embrace it and be changed by it. That is something I could not have discovered or experienced if I had never stepped out on this faith journey. My flashbacks filled with terror began to subside and were eventually replaced with the sweet memories I had stored away.

The time at CornerStone soon ended in early December, leaving me not knowing exactly what to do next. Going back to Zimbabwe was still out of the question for the foreseeable future. The last day of my program, an old friend called and offered me a job with his company for a while. I moved into a little second-floor apartment just a few miles away, with a window that overlooked the small downtown skyline. For the first time in months, I felt at peace.

I'm not sure what next God has for me, but I do know that for today, I am right where I need to be. My life may end up being simple, quiet, and hidden, or God may decide to take me on another wild adventure. Either way, it will be wonderful to me. I will be content knowing that He is with me and that He is all I need.

I miss my children every day, but for today I will wait. When God says "Go," I will go, and if He says "Stay" I will stay, because I have learned that it is my yes to Him that thunders in His throne room. All He asks for is our yes, and that is what I have laid before Him. I have realized I am just along for the ride, and so far, it has been amazing.

Epilogue

I returned to Zimbabwe in January of 2009 to visit Fairfield Children's Homes. The children were all growing healthy and happy, and Project HOPE continues to assist orphans in the surrounding areas. There was a renewed sense of hope in the air. A mother's heart was placed within me the day I saw Benji, Chipo, and Nyarai again. It was like seeing my very own children running into my embrace. At that time, it became clear that I should return to Zimbabwe on a more permanent basis again. I am preparing to move back by September 2009. Please be in prayer for the men, women, and children of Zimbabwe. God has given them a mighty strength to continue the journey out of darkness and into great light.

For current updates from Project HOPE, visit www.hopeofzim.blogspot.com. You may also contact me directly at hopeofzim@gmail.com with any questions or comments. Donations for Project HOPE may be sent to:

CornerStone International
PO Box 192
Wilmore, KY 40390
Memo: Hope of Zim

Printed in the United States
153328LV00001B/2/P